RUDOLF BULTMANN

CASCADE COMPANIONS

The Christian theological tradition provides an embarrassment of riches: from scripture to modern scholarship, we are blessed with a vast and complex theological inheritance. And yet this feast of traditional riches is too frequently inaccessible to the general reader.

The Cascade Companions series addresses the challenge by publishing books that combine academic rigor with broad appeal and readability. They aim to introduce nonspecialist readers to that vital storehouse of authors, documents, themes, histories, arguments, and movements that comprise this heritage with brief yet compelling volumes.

TITLES IN THIS SERIES:

Reading Paul by Michael J. Gorman
Theology and Culture by D. Stephen Long
Creation and Evolution by Tatha Wiley
Theological Interpretation of Scripture by Stephen E. Fowl
Reading Bonhoeffer by Geffrey B. Kelly
Justpeace Ethics by Jarem Sawatsky
Feminism and Christianity by Caryn D. Griswold
Angels, Worms, and Bogeys by Michelle A. Clifton-Soderstrom
Christianity and Politics by C. C. Pecknold
A Way to Scholasticism by Peter S. Dillard
Theological Theodicy by Daniel Castelo
The Letter to the Hebrews in Social-Scientific Perspective
    by David A. deSilva
Basil of Caesarea by Andrew Radde-Galwitz
A Guide to St. Symeon the New Theologian by Hannah Hunt
Reading John by Christopher W. Skinner
Forgiveness by Anthony Bash
Jeremiah by Jack Lundbom
John Calvin by Donald K. McKim
Scripture's Knowing by Dru Johnson
Richard Hooker by W. Bradford Littlejohn

RUDOLF BULTMANN

A Companion to His Theology

DAVID W. CONGDON

CASCADE *Books* • Eugene, Oregon

RUDOLF BULTMANN
A Companion to His Theology

Cascade Books
An Imprint of Wipf and Stock Publishers
199 W. 8th Ave., Suite 3
Eugene, OR 97401
www.wipfandstock.com

ISBN 13: 978-1-62564-748-1

Cataloging-in-Publication data:

Congdon, David W.

　　Rudolf Bultmann: a companion to his theology

　　xx + 176 p. ; cm. Includes bibliographical references.

　　ISBN 13: 978-1-62564-748-1

　　1. Theology 2. Rudolf Bultmann. I. Title.

BX4916 B99 C23 2012

Manufactured in the U.S.A.

For Amy,
who understands me
better than I understand myself

ἄρτι γινώσκω ἐκ μέρους, τότε δὲ ἐπιγνώσομαι καθὼς
καὶ ἐπεγνώσθην

CONTENTS

Acknowledgments • *xi*

Introduction • *xiii*

Abbreviations • *xix*

1 Eschatology • 1

2 Dialectic • 14

3 Nonobjectifiability • 32

4 Self-Understanding • 52

5 Kerygma • 62

6 History • 86

7 Myth • 101

8 Hermeneutics • 112

9 Freedom • 129

10 Advent • 146

Further Reading • *161*

Bibliography • *163*

Subject Index • *171*

ACKNOWLEDGMENTS

THIS BOOK WOULD NOT have happened without the interest of Christian Amondson and the folks at Wipf and Stock. I am grateful to them for their ongoing support of my work. They are more than my partners in publishing; they are friends.

The book has been dramatically improved thanks to the suggestions and corrections of others, including Christophe Chalamet, James F. Kay, and W. Travis McMaken. Not only did they save me from numerous errors, but they also offered insightful suggestions for revision and expansion. My special thanks to Travis McMaken for his friendship and collaboration. I am additionally grateful to John Flett, James Gordon, J. Scott Jackson, Nathaniel Maddox, Bruce McCormack, and Benjamin Myers.

I have been an editor at IVP Academic since 2012, and I could not have asked for a better or more encouraging environment to pursue my own work as a scholar. It has been a blessing to be involved in such stimulating projects, many of which have directly impacted my own work by expanding my conversation partners and broadening my intellectual horizons.

I am deeply thankful for my parents, Jon and Harriet Congdon, and my in-laws, Art and Karen Fong, for their constant assistance over the years. My mother, Harriet, also read through the manuscript and offered very helpful feedback for revision.

Acknowledgments

Most importantly, I have been surrounded and upheld by the love of my children and the tireless support of my wife, Amy, to whom I dedicate this book.

INTRODUCTION

KNOWN FOR HIS WORK in form criticism and his program of demythologizing, Rudolf Bultmann (1884–1976) was arguably the most significant—and certainly the most controversial—New Testament scholar of the twentieth century. Trained in German liberal theology, his study of early Christianity and his experience of the First World War contributed to his early adoption of dialectical theology, with which he identified until the end of his life. He was a passionate opponent of the German Christians and the Nazi regime during the 1930s and 1940s. His main works include *The History of the Synoptic Tradition* (1921), *Jesus and the Word* (1926), *The Gospel of John* (1937–1941), and *Theology of the New Testament* (1948–53). Most of his theological writing, however, takes the form of essays, some of which is collected in the four-volume *Glauben und Verstehen.*[1]

Throughout the 1950s and 1960s, Bultmann was the center of the theological conversation in both Europe and North America. In 1964 *Time* magazine said that "Dr. Rudolf Bultmann's Marburg Disciples . . . dominate German theology the way the Russians rule chess."[2] This state of af-

---

1. The first volume (except for two essays) is translated as *Faith and Understanding.* The second volume is available in English as *Essays Philosophical and Theological.* Only individual essays from the third and fourth volumes are translated.

2. "Existential Way," 86.

fairs could not last, of course. Many of these disciples went on to criticize their teacher in articles and books, while the disciples of rival professors, such as Karl Barth, launched more wide-ranging attacks. The academy suffered Bultmann-fatigue. The hermeneutical talk about the relation between theology and philosophy had become exhausting, so when new movements like narrative theology, political theology, and theology of hope came along, the theological discussions changed almost overnight. Bultmann died in 1976 just as the conversation in North America was turning toward figures like James Cone, Hans Frei, and David Tracy. And despite the important publications about Bultmann during the intervening years, the standard picture of his theology has remained largely static since his death.

Somewhat surprisingly, Rudolf Bultmann is the subject of growing interest again. We can attribute this largely to the publication of documents from his archive in Tübingen. Since the turn of the century, his letters with Friedrich Gogarten, Martin Heidegger, Paul Althaus, and Günther Bornkamm have been published, and many other volumes are in the works. Other recent publications include a volume of his book reviews and a collection of four fairy tales Bultmann wrote for Helene Feldmann in 1916–1917, whom he married in August 1917.[3] In 2009 Konrad Hammann published his masterful biography of Bultmann. It is only natural that these texts should inspire a new generation to read Bultmann with fresh eyes. The goal of this brief guide is to assist these new readers.

First-time readers of Bultmann—especially if they have been introduced to him through a survey textbook or course lecture—tend to have two primary reactions that usually occur simultaneously. The first is surprise at

3. See Bultmann, *Theologie als Kritik*; Bultmann, *Wachen und Träumen*.

discovering that he is not the menacing arch-heretic they were led to believe he was. (A friend of mine, upon finishing the famous programmatic essay on demythologizing for the first time, told me he kept waiting for the sinister demythologizing he had heard so much about but which never arrived. This is not an uncommon reaction.) Indeed, when one reads the vast majority of his writings, and especially his sermons, one is struck by the deep piety and the confident faith in God's revelation. One might even call him *conservative* in his firm adherence to the theology of the Lutheran Reformation. Indeed, he was strongly criticized for this by more liberal theologians who did not understand why he affirmed the exclusive saving significance of Jesus Christ. This brings me to my next point.

The other reaction readers have to Bultmann is perplexity at some of his theological decisions and assertions. He frequently makes claims that seem obvious to him but less than obvious to his readers. His dialectical style of affirming one thing before going on to deny it a few pages later often misleads people who are accustomed to thinkers always asserting what they actually believe. Despite the clarity of Bultmann's writing, one has to be familiar with the underlying network of theological, philosophical, and historical presuppositions in order to interpret his works properly. He is a systematically consistent thinker: he is not only consistent diachronically across the entire span of his academic career, but also consistent synchronically across the entire breadth of his scholarly work—spanning New Testament exegesis, systematic theology, historical research, and hermeneutical methodology. Decisions in one area of his thought cohere with decisions in another area. For this reason, a new student of Bultmann needs to become familiar with the overarching framework of his thought, and that is what this book seeks to provide.

I should say a few words about what this book is *not*. I do not provide in these pages a true introduction to Bultmann. I eschew the usual discussion of biography. There is no historical account of his career to be found in these pages, no contextual description of his main works. Others, especially Hammann, already offer excellent accounts along these lines. While I discuss historical details where appropriate, especially in the opening chapter, this is not intended to serve as a work of intellectual history. What I aim to do instead is to provide an overview of Bultmann's theology through an examination of ten key themes: eschatology, dialectic, nonobjectifiability, self-understanding, kerygma, history, myth, hermeneutics, freedom, and advent. This is by no means an exhaustive list. Many other themes could have been chosen as a way of exploring his thought. I selected these because of their interconnection and their broad usefulness in understanding Bultmann's theology as a systematic whole. The hope is that readers of this companion will be given the conceptual tools to read Bultmann profitably and responsibly on their own. And that is the ultimate aim of this book: to encourage people to set aside the tired stereotypes and overly simplistic textbook summaries and read the great Marburger for themselves.

I encourage those who find their appetites whetted by this book to pick up more advanced works. There is, of course, no shortage of literature on Bultmann, though the vast majority of it is dated and of questionable value. I have included a short list of recommended primary and secondary sources at the end. For those interested in the relation between Bultmann and Barth, or in Bultmann's program of demythologizing, I recommend reading my previous book, *The Mission of Demythologizing: Rudolf Bultmann's Dialectical Theology*.

In 1960, amid the heated discussion around his hermeneutical program, Bultmann wrote:

> It is incredible how many people pass judgment on my work without ever having read a word of it. . . . I have sometimes asked the grounds for a writer's verdict, and which of my writings he has read. The answer has regularly been, without exception, that he has not read any of my writings; but he has learnt from a Sunday paper or a parish magazine that I am a heretic.[4]

If reading the present work induces anyone to pass judgment upon Bultmann without actually reading him, this work has failed. If a reader is to take only one thing away from this book, I hope it will be a sense that Bultmann's theology is complex and significant enough to demand thorough engagement. Many people will, of course, still find Bultmann's theology problematic, no matter how well it is explained. But at the very least we must make the attempt at a charitable reading. Given how he was treated, we owe him that much.

C. S. Lewis's words in *An Experiment in Criticism* on reading works of literature are appropriate here:

> If you already distrust the man you are going to meet, everything he says or does will seem to confirm your suspicions. We can find a book bad only by reading it as if it might, after all, be very good. We must empty our minds and lay ourselves open. There is no work in which holes can't be picked; no work that can succeed without a preliminary act of good will on the part of the reader.[5]

---

4. Quoted in Schmithals, *Introduction*, 20–21.

5. Lewis, *Experiment*, 116.

Bultmann may be wrong, but so too may the great doctors of the church. We must lay ourselves open to all, ancient and modern, the beloved and the despised. Like our reading of the Bible, our reading of Bultmann "must not presuppose its results."[6] If this guide to his theology helps to increase one's act of good will towards him, that is all I can ask or expect.

A NOTE ON TRANSLATION

To make it easier for English-speaking readers to explore Bultmann's writings for themselves, I have tried to cite the best available English translation wherever possible. In many cases, however, I have found those translations deficient. Sometimes I have had to correct the translation to highlight Bultmann's use of a particular term. In almost every case I have made the translations gender neutral or inclusive. I have indicated in the footnote ("rev.") where such revisions have taken place.

6. Bultmann, "Is Exegesis without Presuppositions," 145.

ABBREVIATIONS

CD	*Church Dogmatics*
DT	dialectical theology
GuV	*Glauben und Verstehen*
LW	*Luther's Works*
NT	New Testament
rev.	revised translation
TNT	*Theology of the New Testament*

1

ESCHATOLOGY

INTRODUCTIONS TO RUDOLF BULTMANN, especially in English, tend to approach him by first looking at his hermeneutics, his form- and historical-critical scholarship, or his philosophical influences. They start, that is, with some aspect of epistemology (i.e., the study of knowledge, particularly the question of methodology). This is understandable, given how dominant the subject of epistemology is in modernity—especially in modern theology, as the traditional assumptions and sources of knowledge came under scrutiny—and how crucial it is for Bultmann's own theological work. But as an introduction to Bultmann, as an orientation to the way he thinks and why, it is backwards.

Those who want to understand Bultmann must begin not at the philosophical-hermeneutical-epistemological beginning but at the theological *end*—that is to say, at the doctrine of the end, or eschatology. As a matter of biographical history, Bultmann happened to begin his theological studies at a time when eschatology was being rediscovered after centuries of dismissal and neglect. He entered his training at precisely the right moment: after the significance of eschatology was already recognized, but before it had been theologically integrated and developed. He was thus

1

perfectly positioned to be a pioneer in the eschatological awakening of modern Christianity, which is exactly what he became.

In order to read Bultmann rightly, therefore, the first thing to realize is that he was essentially an *eschatological theologian*. The theme of eschatology was not merely a central topic of his historical and theological writings; it functioned as a norm and criterion that determined his thinking about every theological issue. Every other aspect of Bultmann's theology derives from the fact that he was, from first to last, a theologian of the eschatological reality of God.

THE TURN TO ESCHATOLOGY

In 1959 Rudolf Bultmann wrote a brief article for the *Expository Times* as part of a series on the books that were most important to a particular scholar's thinking. Bultmann listed six books in roughly chronological order. The third book in the list was the second edition of Johannes Weiss's *Die Predigt Jesu vom Reiche Gottes* (ET *Jesus' Proclamation of the Kingdom of God*). Regarding this book, Bultmann wrote: "Here my eyes were opened to the 'eschatological' character of the preaching of Jesus; that is, I saw that the Kingdom of God preached by Him was not a religious and ethical community located within, but a miraculous 'eschatological' entity."[1] To understand the development of Bultmann's theology and hermeneutics, we will need to go back to Weiss and the revolution he initiated in biblical studies.

In early 1892, when the young Bultmann was only seven years old, the Marburg New Testament scholar Johannes Weiss published a short work on the preaching of Jesus about the kingdom of God, which he knew was going

1. Bultmann, "Milestones," 125.

2

to upset a lot of people. The issue is that, at face value, the NT texts indicate that Jesus proclaimed (and his followers believed in) the literal, imminent arrival of a new divine kingdom upon earth within the disciples' lifetime (cf. Matt 10:23). This kingdom, of course, never actually arrived as expected. The early church quickly found ways to reconcile their faith in Jesus as the messiah with this great disappointment. The most famous approach was to claim that "with the Lord one day is like a thousand years" (2 Pet 3:8). Having deferred the eschaton indefinitely, the church lost the eschatological consciousness of the early community and focused on itself, on its liturgy and doctrine, on its relation to the wider culture and the government. Ernst Käsemann calls this transition period "early catholicism."[2] Now that they were no longer expecting the imminent end of history, these early Christians could get on with the business of living in the world. The death of apocalyptic—understood here as the imminent expectation of the messiah's coming—was not the death of eschatology as such, of course. The Christian community continued to believe in and await a future last judgment, along with the coming of God's kingdom for all creation. But the decisive events where salvation was concerned were now all innerworldly; baptism into the church was now the entrance into the new age. Participating in the church replaced waiting for the kingdom.

Everything changed in modernity. Skepticism regarding the nonempirical and the general loss of credence in religious authority created space to question the assumptions regarding eschatology and the afterlife. The speculative hope in a paradisiacal reign at the permanently-deferred end of history could not withstand the Kantian criticism of metaphysics. Immanuel Kant's exclusion of the unintuitable and supratemporal from the realm of reason rendered the

2. Käsemann, *New Testament Questions*, 236–37.

3

traditional doctrine of eschatology no longer credible as an article of belief. For these and other reasons, theologians searched for ways of understanding the biblical language of the kingdom that did not require appeal to the supernatural and the metaphysical. They did not have to search far. There was already a long-standing orthodox tradition of identifying the kingdom of God with the church on earth, based on passages like the "keys of the kingdom" (Matt 16:19). And there was certainly a robust moral tradition inherited from medieval theology. It was easy enough for modern liberal theologians to conclude that talk of God's kingdom in the Bible was actually a metaphorical way of speaking about an idealistic innerhistorical moral community. To belong to the kingdom of God, according to the liberal view, was to adhere to various universal religious and ethical truths. Friedrich Schleiermacher paved the way for this view, but it was Albrecht Ritschl who systematized it.

Weiss was explicitly critical of the liberal position, but this placed him in an uncomfortable position, given that Ritschl was his father-in-law. While Weiss delayed the publication of his book until 1892 to avoid personally upsetting Ritschl, he explicitly addressed his book to those who held Ritschl's views, which included himself. Weiss exposed the liberal position as an illegitimate imposition of a Kantian framework upon the biblical text. The early Christian community did not use this language symbolically. They genuinely believed in the imminent arrival of God's messianic reign within their lifetimes. To be sure, Weiss considered such a notion delusional, and so he posed the fundamental challenge for future theologians: to translate the content of the New Testament into the context of the contemporary world. Or as Weiss put it, theologians today must "issue the old coinage at a new rate of exchange."[3] I will return to this

3. Weiss, *Die Predigt Jesu*, 7.

hermeneutical challenge later, when I discuss Bultmann's program of demythologizing. For now all we need to see is that Weiss set the stage for later scholars, who came along and developed his insight into the eschatological nature of the early Christian gospel.

Bultmann began his theological studies in 1903 at Tübingen University. He then went to Berlin in 1904 before arriving, in 1905, at Marburg University, the goal and climax of his education. There he came under the influence of Adolf Jülicher, Paul Natorp, Wilhelm Herrmann, and, especially, Weiss. By this point, the latter's thesis regarding the eschatological orientation of Jesus was widely accepted. The following year, in 1906, Albert Schweitzer published his groundbreaking *Von Reimarus zu Wrede: Eine Geschichte der Leben-Jesu-Forschung*, later translated as *The Quest of the Historical Jesus*. Schweitzer's work not only radicalized Weiss's thesis about Jesus' preaching, but it had the additional effect of bringing the quest for the historical Jesus to a screeching halt.[4]

Bultmann was thus trained within a context that recognized the thoroughly eschatological nature of early Christianity but had no idea what to do with this insight theologically. In the lectures he gave in 1951 at Yale University and Vanderbilt University,[5] published as *Jesus Christ and Mythology* in 1958, Bultmann recalls the "epoch-making" significance of Weiss: "Weiss showed that the Kingdom of God is not immanent in the world and does not grow as part of the world's history, but is rather eschatological;

4. For more on Schweitzer and Bultmann, see Grässer, "Albert Schweitzer und Rudolf Bultmann," 53–69.

5. These lectures were given at the height of the controversy over his program of demythologizing, which he had announced in 1941. Indeed, in 1951 Bultmann was being subjected to various heresy trials by the Protestant church in Germany, which mostly ceased by the following year. See Hammann, *Rudolf Bultmann*, 443–48.

i.e., the Kingdom of God transcends the historical order. It will come into being not through the moral endeavour of man, but solely through the supernatural action of God."[6] Bultmann then recounts the words of his professor in Berlin, Julius Kaftan, who said that "if Johannes Weiss is right and the conception of the Kingdom of God is an eschatological one, then it is impossible to make use of this conception in dogmatics."[7] One person who agreed with Kaftan was Wilhelm Herrmann, the much beloved professor of both Bultmann and Karl Barth. When faced with the truth of Weiss's presentation of early Christian eschatology, Herrmann retreated from talking of God's kingdom and focused instead on "the personal experience of revelation."[8] Or rather he reinterpreted the language of the kingdom to refer to the "inner life" of Jesus himself, safe from the problems of history.[9]

Like many others, Bultmann soon found this way of resolving the conundrum unsatisfactory. For one thing it was an escape from the real challenge and claim posed by the biblical text. The tragedy of the First World War also had the effect of making eschatology existentially relevant once again.[10] But it was not until he encountered the work

6. Bultmann, *Jesus Christ*, 12.

7. Ibid., 13.

8. Chalamet, *Dialectical Theologians*, 46.

9. Herrmann, *Communion*, 60–61: "In the Christian fellowship we are made acquainted, not merely with the external course of Jesus' lot in life and of His work in history, but we are led into His presence and receive a picture of His inner life. . . . We need communion with Christians in order that, from the picture of Jesus which His church has preserved, there may shine forth that inner life which is the heart of it. . . . Thus we would never apprehend the most important element in the historical appearance of Jesus did not His people make us feel it."

10. "When *The Quest of the Historical Jesus* was written, the eschatological orientation of Jesus' and primitive Christianity's

of Friedrich Gogarten and Karl Barth in 1919–1920 that he saw a new way forward: an understanding of Christian faith and theology that embraced the eschatological character of the early Christian gospel under the conditions of the modern age.

ESCHATOLOGY WITHOUT APOCALYPTIC

In the second edition of his commentary on Romans, Barth made what was at that time a surprising claim: "Christianity that is not completely and utterly eschatology has completely and utterly nothing to do with *Christ*."[11] But in that same commentary, Barth explicitly denies holding to any literal apocalyptic vision of the coming kingdom, which he calls "enthusiastic-apocalyptic illusions of an anticipated unity of the immanent and the transcendent."[12] Whatever eschatology means, it cannot refer to some future occurrence in which the "Son of Man" comes down from the clouds, as if God lives in some ethereal abode in what we now call outer space. While apocalyptic in that sense has died, this does not mean that we are necessarily bereft of an eschatological hope, though such hope will have to look very different than it once did.

Barth thus differentiates between *apocalyptic* (understood as the belief in a literal future *parousia*) and *eschatology* (understood as the present actualization of and

---

message could only bewilder contemporary theology. But for theology after World War I, which no longer understood itself in terms of cultural optimism, but more nearly apocalyptically (*The Decline of the West*), Schweitzer's discovery provided an orientation for the new understanding of existence." James M. Robinson, introduction to Schweitzer, *Quest of the Historical Jesus*, xxi.

11. Barth, *Römerbrief*, 430.

12. Ibid., 225.

encounter with the eschaton).[13] It was this distinction that showed Bultmann how to remain in theological contact with the biblical text without abandoning his modern context. With the liberals Bultmann acknowledged the alien character of the biblical texts, but against the liberals Bultmann affirmed that these texts remain significant for our faith and practice today *precisely in their eschatological character*. He was able to recognize as a historian that *what* the early Christians hoped for proved to be mistaken, while also recognizing that the *expectation itself* is, in some sense, essential to the faith.

While it took a number of years to finally reach its mature form, this distinction between apocalyptic and eschatology eventually turned into Bultmann's distinction between mythological and nonmythological modes of God-talk. We will look at the concept of myth in more depth later, but it is important to point out now that Bultmann's approach to myth is fundamentally determined by his attempt to make sense of primitive apocalyptic thought in the New Testament, given the fact that, for modern Christians, "mythological eschatology has passed away."[14] In *Jesus Christ and Mythology*, after introducing the problem posed by the nonoccurrence of the *parousia*, Bultmann poses the central

13. The concept of "apocalyptic" is ambiguous, due to the fact that it can name a literary genre *and* an intellectual movement. As a literary genre it names various works written in the period of Second Temple Judaism, including Daniel, 1 Enoch, 2 Baruch, 4 Ezra, and the Apocalypse of John. Among these works we find identifying markers, such as the revelation of secret mysteries, visions and seers, and symbolic imagery. As an intellectual-historical movement, we have to differentiate between at least Jewish-prophetic and early Christian apocalyptic, but in general we find common themes like an imminent end of history, cosmic catastrophe, the enthronement of God or the Son of God, otherworldly agents and powers, and the coming of salvation. For more on this, see Koch, *Rediscovery of Apocalyptic*, 18–35.

14. Bultmann, *Jesus Christ*, 25.

challenge for theologians today: "We must ask whether the eschatological preaching and the mythological sayings as a whole contain a still deeper meaning which is concealed under the cover of mythology. If that is so, let us abandon the mythological conceptions precisely because we want to retain their deeper meaning."[15] The task for theology, according to Bultmann, is to discern this "deeper meaning"—a task he calls "demythologizing." With respect to biblical apocalyptic, Bultmann interprets the expected end of the world as referring to "the judgment of God" upon humankind for turning the world "into a place in which evil spreads and sin rules." This divine judgment "calls men first and foremost to responsibility toward God and to repentance. It calls them to perform the will of God."[16]

In his pursuit of this deeper meaning in the New Testament, Bultmann seeks to answer the question: *what truth comes to expression in primitive Christian apocalyptic that does not depend upon (and can be differentiated from) the ancient conception of the cosmos?* This ancient conception comprises, among other things, the intervention of supernatural forces in everyday occurrences, the enslavement of the cosmos to competing supernatural powers and principalities, and the imminent destruction of the cosmos as part of the arrival of the new cosmic order. Put simply, if their view of the cosmic order was flawed, what was the truth in the ancient community's theology that remains relevant for people who no longer believe—and no longer *have* to believe—that illness, evil, and suffering are the work of evil spirits or that a divine messiah is going to appear to restore world order? We will never understand Bultmann's theological project if we do not realize that *this* is the fundamental question underpinning his work from

15. Ibid., 18.
16. Ibid., 26.

beginning to end. Attempts to approach Bultmann's theology as if it were a program for integrating philosophy and theology inevitably miss the point. They fail to see that one is compelled to ask Bultmann's questions entirely within the terms of the New Testament, read in light of its historical context as a document that seeks to make sense of the early community's confidence in the imminent advent of Christ.

THE CHALLENGE OF READING BULTMANN

Reading Bultmann today is made difficult not only because of these faulty assumptions about his own project, but also because of simplistic dismissals of the problem posed by early apocalyptic eschatology. Following the rediscovery of eschatology, scholars split into two camps: those who advocated a present, realized eschatology (Bultmann, Dodd), and those who retained in some form the imminent, future eschatology of the early church (Käsemann, Pannenberg, Moltmann). Beginning in the mid-twentieth century, conservative scholars found an easy way out of this debate with a classic "both-and" approach, which goes by the name "inaugurated eschatology." Associated originally with Werner Kümmel, the position was popularized within anglophone evangelical circles initially by George Eldon Ladd and today by N. T. Wright. The position is immensely attractive for obvious reasons: it allows one to affirm both the future and present eschatological passages in the NT while avoiding issues of historical context and theological conflict. All problems immediately disappear. Today the phrase "already but not yet" is a theological truism. But its near-universal acceptance means that readers of Bultmann today are likely to find themselves confounded by the way he sets up the task of theology in terms of an eschatological dilemma that most people no longer think exists. We are now conditioned to ignore statements about the disciples not tasting death before they see the kingdom of God (Mark 9:1; Matt 16:28; Luke 9:27), or perhaps treating it as an intentional statement of hyperbole, or as a reference to seeing the resurrected Christ, or some other interpretation. We assume that the coming kingdom was always supposed to appear in the distant future. The short-lived idea that it was going to arrive in the near future was just an overly enthusiastic anomaly, but it was never really taken seriously.

These and other similar ideas are fairly widespread today. The reason is obvious: We are deeply uncomfortable with the idea that the people whose views we hold to be authoritative, perhaps even infallible, might have held ideas that were simply wrong or at least profoundly alien to our own way of thinking. We are afraid that, if they were wrong about the imminent *parousia*, they might be wrong about other things more essential to the faith. It is only natural to look for explanations that close up these loopholes and shore up the faith against doubt. But in doing so, many Christians have inoculated themselves against the problems and dilemmas posed by the biblical text and the history of ancient Christianity. Moreover, this strategy secures the faith at the cost of recognizing just how truly *strange* and *other* the biblical world is. The danger in denying the cultural and historical otherness of the text is that we risk creating an environment in which cultural and theological differences are seen as a *threat* to the faith. We start to see multiple viewpoints and divergent interpretations not as an intrinsic part of the diverse body of believers but as a menace to the (idolatrous) security of "knowing" that our way is the right way, that our thoughts are God's thoughts.

An alternative and increasingly popular approach is to recognize the strangeness of the Bible but to insist that becoming a Christian requires that we abandon our present

11

world in order to inhabit the biblical world. This approach has the advantage of acknowledging the historical otherness of scripture, which encourages, at least in theory, good historical scholarship. But this position only repeats the same mistake by assuming that whatever cultural world Jesus and Paul inhabit, it has to be *my* cultural world as well. So if they belonged to an apocalyptic-mythological context, then that also must become my intellectual context, regardless of what that might entail. The common (and mistaken) presupposition is that my conceptuality has to be the same as that of the NT. Never mind the fact there is contextual and conceptual divergence *within* the NT itself.[17] What is at issue here is the purported inseparability of the *message* of the Bible from its cultural-historical *context*. Upholding this inseparability is yet another way of denying that plurality is intrinsic to the faith, though denying it can lead to other dangers, especially if we conclude that the gospel message exists in a purely acultural form. Between the reductionist Scylla and the abstract Charybdis lies the path of Bultmann, which requires that we "let all security go" and "enter into inner darkness," and few have such faith.[18]

Reading Bultmann responsibly requires that we open ourselves to the alien character of the Bible. It also challenges us to take this strange world seriously, in all its historical complexity, without thereby assuming that we must somehow make this strange world our own. How this is possible is the task undertaken by hermeneutical theology, which is to say, by all genuine theology that grapples with the problem posed by the dissonance between the world of the text and the world of the reader. Subsequent chapters will explore Bultmann's way of handling this problem. His

17. Matters become still more problematic when we take the Old Testament into account.

18. Bultmann, "On the Problem," 122.

way may not be or become our own, but we cannot make sense of his work if we do not first see the validity and necessity of taking on this task.

QUESTIONS FOR REFLECTION

1. What is the eschaton?

2. What does it mean to believe in the "return" or "second coming" of Christ? Can Christianity withstand the loss of belief in Christ's literal return? If so, how might we interpret the creed's confession that Christ will come to judge the living and the dead?

3. How does one reconcile eschatological hope with the scientific expectation of a dying sun swallowing up the earth?

4. Is eschatology more than wishful thinking? If so, in what sense?

5. Can belief in the authority of scripture coexist with the claim that the biblical authors were wrong about certain points, some of which were held in high importance (e.g., the imminent return)?

2

DIALECTIC

BULTMANN'S INTEREST IN ESCHATOLOGY placed him, at least in part, in the camp of the liberals and modernists, insofar as it forced him to grapple with the culturally relative nature of the biblical texts. The rediscovery of ancient apocalyptic was also the rediscovery of the cultural distance between the early Christian community and the contemporary church. That would come to play an important role in his later hermeneutics, as we will see in future chapters. If Bultmann had let this fact determine his theology, then he almost certainly would have been a liberal theologian like Johannes Weiss or Albert Schweitzer. But in 1920 Bultmann came under the influence of the new "dialectical theology" (hereafter DT) of Karl Barth and Friedrich Gogarten, which balanced out cultural difference with theological nearness.[1]

1. Some often refer to this as "neoorthodox" theology, but that term is mistakenly applied to Barth and should be abandoned: he is neither "orthodox" in the sense of repristinating traditional orthodoxy, nor is he "neo" in the sense of establishing a new orthodoxy all his own. The term "neoorthodoxy" is an Anglo-American creation that Barth explicitly opposed; the theologians actually involved in the movement referred to their project as "dialectical theology," so that is the term we should use.

But what exactly defines DT? This question admits no easy answer, given the diverse range of views held by those who claimed the label. In addition to Barth, Bultmann, and Gogarten, the original school of DT included Eduard Thurneysen and Emil Brunner, and one could add the early Paul Tillich to this list as well. In any case, this is not the place to attempt a comprehensive answer to this question.[2] I will instead look at the context of Bultmann's turn to DT and his subsequent definition of the term within his own work. We will see that, for Bultmann, DT was the natural extension of his insight into the eschatological character of early Christianity, but it enabled this ancient eschatology to become theologically meaningful and productive within the contemporary situation. Thanks to DT, eschatology was not just a historical problem posed by the biblical text; it became, instead, the basis for a new approach to thinking and speaking about God.

BULTMANN'S TURN TO DIALECTICAL THEOLOGY

Unlike Barth, Bultmann did not abandon liberal theology primarily as a result of the experience of the war or a disillusionment with his theological teachers. He was instead convinced on exegetical and theological grounds that the theology of his teachers was lacking in certain crucial respects, and this seems to have occurred as part of his doctoral and postdoctoral studies. His research in early Christianity gave him a keen awareness of where modern liberal theology had departed from the primitive Christian community in ways that were historically impossible or theologically inadequate. What was missing was a theology that could replace liberalism by integrating the turn to eschatology under the

2. I have done so already in Congdon, *Mission*, chaps. 2–3.

conditions of modernity. Bultmann encountered just such a theology in the work of Barth and Gogarten.

Bultmann was not immediately convinced by the new theology. His reading of the first edition of Barth's *Epistle to the Romans* (*Der Römerbrief*) did not impress him. In a lecture in Eisenach in 1920, Bultmann publicly criticized both Barth and liberal theology.[3] He conceptualized both theologies using Wilhelm Bousset's distinction between Palestinian and Hellenistic Christianity.[4] Bousset differentiates between the ethical religion of the original Jesus-community, which was a sect within Judaism, and the mythical-mystical religion of the later Hellenistic community, which became the home of Pauline Christianity. Bultmann associates Barth—along with the piety "operative in the church"[5]—with the mythical religion of Hellenism and associates liberal theology, with its quests for the pre-Pauline "historical Jesus," with the ethical religion of Palestine.[6] According to Bultmann, the Barth of the first *Romans* commentary repristinates the Pauline Christ-myth, while the liberals fabricate a historically-reconstructed Jesus that has nothing to do with genuine Christianity. In neither case do we have what Bultmann understands as true religion, which "has to do with the reality of receiving oneself through divine grace, with being transformed, with being created anew to a nature whose activity is not the fulfillment of a demand but the presentation of its being."[7] He concludes by stating that "what is decisive for religion is neither the cultic and mythical means of expression, nor the psychic conditions in which the pious experience God,

3. See Bultmann, "Ethical."

4. See Bousset, *Kyrios Christos*.

5. Bultmann, "Ethical," 224.

6. Ibid., 230–31.

7. Ibid., 233–34.

but only a religion's spiritual content, the reality which it characterizes as God." What matters is not one's subjective experiences, doctrinal beliefs, or liturgical practices, but "only whether he can speak of a revelation of God, whether he has found God as a reality which subdues and blesses him, a reality in which he finds the meaning of his life."[8] Bultmann is thus looking for a theology that (a) speaks of *God* and not merely of human beings and also (b) remains responsibly connected to the historical kerygma (or gospel) of early Christianity.[9]

In 1920 Bultmann commends an alternative to both Barth and liberalism, namely, the work of Gogarten, particularly his 1917 book, *Religion weither* (Religion from afar).[10] And as important as Gogarten was and remained throughout Bultmann's life, what really sealed his turn to DT was the publication in early 1922 of the second edition of Barth's *Epistle to the Romans*. Here he encountered a work that fulfilled his conditions, not always ideally but in a way that was so constructive and compelling as to enable him truly to break with the liberal theology of his upbringing and embrace a new mode of theological existence. Bultmann thus placed the second *Epistle to the Romans* on his list of the five most personally significant books, writing: "From this book it became decisively clear to me (1) that the essence of Christian faith does not consist in an attitude of the soul, but in its relation to its object, God's revelation; and (2) that the interpretation of a text presupposes a

8. Ibid., 235.

9. I devote a later chapter to the topic of the kerygma (see chap. 5). In one sense it functions as a synonym for "gospel," but Bultmann uses it to highlight the distinctive message of the earliest Christian community. The kerygma is the message *about* Jesus as the Christ that the early Christians proclaimed and translated into scripture.

10. Bultmann, "Ethical," 230.

personal relation to the matter of which the text speaks."[11] We will look at the second point in detail later, when we take up the question of Bultmann's hermeneutics. At present we need to explore further the first point.

DIALECTICAL THEOLOGY AS EXISTENTIAL THEOLOGY

In the mid-1920s, Bultmann wrote several key essays that attempted not only to give a scholarly assessment of DT but also to contribute to this new theological movement. Though Bultmann thought Barth's theological instincts were basically right, the two of them had important disagreements about the relation between revelation and scripture, about which they corresponded in 1922–24. This back-and-forth exchange resulted in Barth writing an important preface to the third edition of his Romans commentary, and it led Bultmann to give some key lectures on DT as it relates to liberal theology and New Testament scholarship. In Eisenach in October 1927 he gave perhaps the most important of these lectures, this time on "The Significance of 'Dialectical Theology' for the Scientific Study of the New Testament." This essay gives us the best insight into why Bultmann identified himself with DT and what role it plays in his theology.

Bultmann opens the lecture by disabusing his listeners of two misunderstandings about DT: first, that DT is a timeless theological system; and, second, that DT is a timeless theological method.

> The designation "dialectical theology" does *not* refer to a *theological system* presenting particular formulations of dogma which might be relevant for New Testament study—such as statements

11. Bultmann, "Milestones," 125.

> about sin and grace, revelation and Christ—and
> might be deduced from a dogmatic principle. . . .
> Nor, however, does the term "dialectical theol-
> ogy" denote a *method of investigation* which
> ought to displace, say, the historical method.[12]

These opening paragraphs can be perplexing to a person not already familiar with Bultmann's way of thinking, and whose knowledge of DT is likely shaped by Barth's writings. Surely, one might say, what else is DT if not an alternative theological method or system? Matters may become still more confusing when Bultmann dismisses the idea that DT sets up "the radical antithesis between God and humanity" as a dogmatic principle and even says that "the statement, 'God is not human and the human is not God,' is not a theological statement in any sense."[13] The latter phrase is a near-direct quotation of Barth's famous early statement that "God is God."[14]

For Bultmann, DT is not a specific *kind* of theology alongside other kinds (e.g., Augustinian, Thomistic, Luther-an, etc.), but rather a statement about the nature of theology itself. The problem with a claim like "God is God and we are not" or "God is merciful to the sinner"[15] is not that it is false but that it "speaks of God *in general* in contrast to humanity *in general*. . . . It therefore does not speak of God; it speaks of the *concept* of God."[16] What DT rejects is not a certain proposition or criterion within theology, but rather a cer-tain way of thinking about theology as such, namely, one that speaks about the *concept* of God rather than the *reality* of God. In contrast to a philosophical notion of dialectic, as

12. Bultmann, "Significance," 145–46.

13. Ibid., rev.

14. See Busch, "God Is God."

15. Bultmann, "Significance," 147.

16. Ibid., 146, rev.

in the Socratic dialogues, dialectic within DT means that "the concept of truth is not determined by the concept of true statement but by the concept of reality."[17] According to Bultmann, the problem with so much theology, especially Protestant theology since the seventeenth century (which is Bultmann's primary concern), is that it has concerned itself with formulating true statements that are supposed to be timelessly and universally valid. But since truth cannot be found in general statements but only in reality—a claim we will explore in more detail below and in later chapters—theology done in this manner does not actually speak of God. Protestant scholasticism represents the most extreme version of this, but the charge applies just as much to liberal theology. Bultmann stated as much three years earlier in his February 1924 lecture on liberal theology, where he said that "the subject of theology is *God*, and the chief charge to be brought against liberal theology is that it has dealt not with God but with humanity."[18]

By dealing instead with the reality of God, and not with a human concept of God, DT approaches the task of theology in a completely different light. The actual theological statements themselves may not be dramatically different, but the way they are understood and interpreted will be. Bultmann uses the example of the claim that "God is merciful to the sinner." Scholasticism might analyze how this idea coheres with other theological and philosophical claims, and a dialectical method might balance this idea with the claim that God also judges the sinner, which, as Bultmann admits, is also true.[19] But those are not theological claims, because they do not actually speak of God. Within DT, by contrast, the statement that God is merciful to the sinner

17. Ibid., 146–47.
18. Bultmann, "Liberal Theology," 29, rev.
19. Bultmann, "Significance," 148.

is "not a general assertion about the concept of God, but declares that the real God is really merciful to real sinners, to you and to me."[20] Theologically speaking, a statement becomes genuinely dialectical when it refers to a reality that we encounter, something that actually affects and transforms us. "God is merciful to the sinner" has to become "God is merciful *to me*." The purpose of theology is to bring to speech the actual event in which one encounters the living God. Theology must do so, of course, through statements that make use of philosophical concepts, but the criterion of their truthfulness is to be found not in their systematic coherence or their consistent application of a method, but in the way the words themselves confront the reader with the reality of God. Within DT, therefore, theology is understood as a mode of proclamation. DT abolishes the separation between systematic and practical theology, which is to say, the separation between God-talk that is generally valid and God-talk that is valid for a particular time and place. Whereas in most traditional accounts of theology, a true theological statement has to be true for everyone and at all times, DT denies this and insists instead that the truth of a statement "applies to the specific time of the speaking."[21] According to Bultmann, true knowledge of divine grace is "not knowledge of a timeless truth or of a fact of the past; it is the acceptance of the gracious act of God."[22] Knowledge of God is identical and coterminous with faith. Theology is dialectical, therefore, insofar as it is *existential*.

A word of clarification is in order. Many critics of Bultmann point to his existential understanding of theology as a chief reason to abandon his version of DT. Even if they do not associate it with Heidegger's existentialist

20. Ibid., 147.
21. Ibid.
22. Ibid., 148.

philosophy (though most do), they still charge it with reducing faith and theology to the individual. They object to Bultmann's emphasis on God's relation to *me*, assuming that he starts with individualism as a premise. What these critics misunderstand is that his focus on the individual is a consequence of his focus on the encounter with the reality of God. Bultmann takes it for granted that only individuals have encounters. No matter how strong one's sense of communal identity, the community itself is not a corporate person that can relate to God in the place of particular persons, at least not in the sense that a person could claim to know God without having been personally affected by God.[23] The theologian who would speak of God's grace can only do so on the basis of God's gracious action *towards her*. Theology speaks out of *this* individual, existential reality, and is for this reason necessarily existential in its understanding of God.

One might very well ask why we should accept Bultmann's understanding of theology. Just because he views theology differently does not necessarily mean it is the right view to hold. For the most part, Bultmann speaks as if his presuppositions are self-evident, and so we must tease them out. For Bultmann, there are two basic reasons. The first is that the person who speaks of God is situated within a historical context, meaning that theology is always dependent upon the particular situation of the theologian. DT uniquely recognizes "the historical nature of speaking about God."[24] We will look at this point in later chapters, when we take up the question of history and the problem of hermeneutics.

23. This position takes for granted a Protestant perspective on faith, over against the medieval Catholic doctrine of "implicit faith" (*fides implicita*), which holds that an individual can implicitly believe whatever the church believes.

24. Bultmann, "Significance," 149.

But there is a second, more important reason for embracing DT, having to do with "the peculiar character of the object" of theology, which "makes [theology] possible."[25] What makes DT necessary as a description of theology as such is the particular character of God.

GOD THE WHOLLY OTHER

The idea of God as "wholly other" did not originate with Barth—that distinction belongs to Rudolf Otto, in his 1917 book on *The Idea of the Holy*—but it became synonymous with him. Not only does Barth use the term many times in the second edition of his *Epistle to the Romans* and in lectures from that period, but he captured the essence of the concept in his famous claim from the commentary's preface that "if I have a system, it is limited to a recognition of what Kierkegaard called the 'infinite qualitative distinction' between time and eternity, and to my regarding this as possessing negative as well as positive significance: 'God is in heaven, and thou art on earth.'"[26]

Bultmann is widely associated with Barth's early theology of the "infinite qualitative distinction," and for good reason. His work consistently emphasizes God's otherness, and the distinction between immanence and transcendence, between the historical and the eschatological, forms the basis for his later hermeneutical program. In an important 1925 essay, "What Does It Mean to Speak of God?" he says that it is "essential to the concept of God that God is the 'Wholly Other.'"[27] But in what sense and on what grounds is God wholly other? According to Bultmann, the meaning of the claim that God is wholly other "is understood only

25. Ibid.
26. Barth, *Epistle*, 10.
27. Bultmann, "What Does It Mean," 55.

in relation to the primary statement that God is the reality that determines our existence."[28] The phrase "determines our existence" is Bultmann's way of describing salvation or justification; to be justified by grace is to have our existence determined by a transcendent reality outside of ourselves. To say that God is wholly other thus means that God is holy and just, the one who judges and justifies:

> The statement that the God who determines my existence is nevertheless the "Wholly Other" can only have the meaning that as *the* "Wholly Other" God confronts me who am a sinner. . . . To speak of God as the "Wholly Other" has meaning, then, only if I have understood that the actual situation of the human person is the situation of the sinner who wants to speak of God and cannot.[29]

God's otherness is therefore a function of God's saving power. It is a function, in other words, of God's gracious relation toward us.

It is crucial, in Bultmann's perspective, to connect transcendence with grace. If we detach God's otherness from God's saving nearness—and not just a general nearness, as in pan(en)theism, but a particular nearness to *me* as a reality that I encounter—then talk of God as wholly other "can only mean that God is *something* wholly different from humanity, a metaphysical being, a kind of an immaterial world, perhaps of a complex of mysterious forces, . . . or finally, *the Irrational*." Every such understanding of God is really talk of a "pseudo-god" whose promises of freedom are a "fraud," because all such concepts are "human abstractions," meaning they start with some quality

28. Ibid., 56.
29. Ibid., 57–58, rev.

or factor in humanity and extrapolate a concept of God.[30] Humanity is material and knowable and historical, so god becomes something immaterial and unknowable and ahistorical. But then the "Wholly Other" is nothing other than what Jacques Lacan would call the "big Other"—namely, an idealized projection and presupposition of the self.[31] Such a god does not exist.

We are now in the position to understand one of Bultmann's most controversial claims: "It is therefore clear that if one wishes to speak of God, one must evidently *speak of oneself.*"[32] Many have appealed to this statement as evidence that Bultmann reduces theology to anthropology, that God in his theology is not truly transcendent and other. Most of these criticisms fail to understand that, in making this claim, Bultmann is actually protecting the genuine otherness of God and the irreducibility of theology to anthropology! As we saw above, Bultmann understands theology to be a way of thinking and speaking about the reality of God that encounters us and so determines our existence. The theologian speaks out of *this* gracious and justifying encounter. From this starting point—and *only* from this starting point—the theologian learns that God is wholly other and that the human person is a sinner, among other things. Theology is therefore existential, in Bultmann's account, meaning that "in speaking of God theology must *at the same time* speak of the human person."[33] The phrase "at the same time" is often overlooked. Bultmann does *not* say that we can reduce God to the human person. He says, in fact, that "no speaking of ourselves can ever be a speaking

30. Ibid., 57, rev.

31. See Lacan, *The Ego*, 235.

32. Bultmann, "What Does It Mean," 55, rev.

33. Bultmann, "Significance," 148, rev. Emphasis mine.

of God, because it speaks only of the human person."[34] And yet, conversely, "no speaking in which we detach ourselves from our own concrete existence is a speaking of God."[35] Trying to speak *about* God in a way that is detached from our existence is an attempt to speak from a neutral, ahistorical, universal position that does not exist. We can only speak from within our own life context. Claiming to speak in a nonexistential manner about God only means that we are speaking about a "pseudo-god." For this reason, "talking of God, *if* it were possible, would necessarily be talking at the same time of ourselves."[36] Talking *at the same time* of both God and ourselves—of God as the one who determines our existence, and of ourselves as those whose existence has been determined by God—is to engage in DT as Bultmann understands it.[37]

SOVEREIGNTY AND FREE WILL: A CASE STUDY

How might it look to put DT into practice? Can DT help resolve theological problems and advance the church's theological dialogue? I propose to illustrate how DT might function practically by using the classic problem of the relation between divine sovereignty and human free will.

The problem of free will is as old as Christianity itself and I will not attempt to summarize every facet of the issue here. The position of classical theism is that God is all-knowing (omniscient), all-powerful (omnipotent), and

34. Bultmann, "What Does It Mean," 56, rev.

35. Ibid., 55–56.

36. Ibid., 60–61.

37. Bultmann's approach is not particularly novel, at least not within the tradition of the Reformation. Calvin himself begins his *Institutes of the Christian Religion* with the two axioms: "without knowledge of self there is no knowledge of God" and "without knowledge of God there is no knowledge of self" (Calvin, *Institutes*, 1.1.1–2).

all-determining (omnicausal), fully sovereign in every dimension of creation. God not only predestines the life of each person but controls every whim of the natural order, all according to God's eternal, though hidden, will. Classical theists resolve the problem of divine sovereignty and human free will by adopting a position known as compatibilism, according to which a human agent is free so long as she is able to do what she wants without coercion or impediment.[38] Incompatibilists argue that this is not a sufficient account of human freedom, because the traditional assumptions regarding divine foreknowledge and causality mean the human agent could not act otherwise; classical theism only allows for the semblance of free will. Others argue that classical theism does not allow for genuinely random occurrences, something that would seem to be required both by modern science and by general human experience. For this reason, incompatibilist theologians have argued for modifications of classical theism, and sometimes even its abandonment. Open theology, for example, rejects exhaustive foreknowledge; the future is as open for God as it is for human creatures.

Instead of going any deeper into the rabbit hole of the free will debate, let us consider how Bultmann might approach the topic on the basis of DT. First of all, Bultmann would find the overall philosophical debate over whether divine sovereignty and human free will are compatible to be nontheological, and that is because all of it remains abstract talk *about* God as a neutral, external object. The debate is a logical problem that has existential implications, to be sure,

38. There are other versions of classical theism, of course. Molinism (or middle knowledge), for example, argues that God has exhaustive foreknowledge of the contingent future (i.e., counterfactuals), and that God decides what to create based on this knowledge of what would freely occur based on a certain person being in a certain situation.

but is not itself existential in nature. The debate over free will presupposes that theology makes general, universal claims that apply to each person in the abstract, what people commonly refer to as a worldview. Bultmann's approach to DT denies this. Christian theology is never properly in the business of articulating and debating worldviews. For him, the problem of sovereignty and free will cannot be decided at the level of logical propositions and general statements. God is not sovereign in general but rather sovereign over *me* and my existence in the world—and, by extension, over *you* and *us*. At the same time, God's sovereignty has a very specific shape and content. The sovereign will of God is a will that places a *demand* upon me. We encounter this demand in the word of God:

> Jesus brings, not rites and practices, but the Word. And he brings the Word, not as a teaching about God, a worldview, but as a call to repentance before the coming kingdom of God. He proclaims the will of God. His Word is summons, a call to decision. . . . The hearing, therefore, is not a mere physical act; it is obedience which entails action. Those who hear and do nothing, who are like the man building on sand, have really not heard at all, although they have ears. For the Word of God is the will of God. . . . The Word alone, as it confronts the hearer in the summons, demands decision. This Word has the power which belongs to the will of God.[39]

The will and word of God claims and summons me, and it summons me precisely as a free agent who necessarily responds. Sovereignty and free will are, on this understanding, paradoxically identical; they occur together simultaneously. The one is impossible without the other. God is only

39. Bultmann, "Concept," 291–92.

sovereign in relation to my free response to the word. And I am only free as the one who has been summoned by God. This is what Bultmann means when he says that we can only talk of God if we talk at the same time of ourselves.

BEYOND LIBERAL AND DIALECTICAL

Returning now to where we began, it is important to see that this existential understanding of theology follows from the eschatology that Bultmann found so attractive in Barth's *Romans*. According to Barth, the eschaton does not lie horizontally ahead of us on the plane of world history but instead intersects and encounters the person of faith vertically from above on the plane of individual existence. The eschatological reign of Christ confronts us not in history (i.e., the observable past) but in what Bultmann calls our *historicity* (i.e., the existential present). If the object of theology is the eschatological inbreaking of God in Jesus Christ, and if this eschatological event is an inherently existential encounter, then it follows that talk of God is necessarily also talk of oneself as the person taken up into this encounter. For this reason, Barth and Bultmann understand the eschatological event as both revelation and reconciliation: it is the event that simultaneously justifies the sinner and communicates true knowledge of God.

Barth would eventually change his mind about this eschatology. In his later dogmatic writings, he grounds the eschaton, and so theology, in the historical person of Jesus, and thus replaces existential theology with a certain kind of christocentric theology.[40] Bultmann, however, consistently

40. We should be careful not to speak as if the term "christocentric" belongs exclusively to the later Barth. Bultmann is christocentric as well, in his own way. He just has a different christology at the center than Barth.

develops the theology of Barth's *Romans*. As Bruce Mc-Cormack observes, "the amount of agreement expressed by Bultmann with Barth's eschatology of the *hic et nunc* [here and now] cannot be missed. In a real sense, Bultmann was the heir to this perspective and remained faithful to it long after Barth had abandoned it."[41]

If Bultmann remains faithful to the theological position of the early Barth, then it follows that he remains a *dialectical* theologian, even in his later work. But this does not mean he is necessarily opposed to everything associated with "liberal" theology. Indeed, it was precisely his faithfulness to a particular dialectical theology that led him to take up ideas and approaches often labeled "liberal," such as existentialism. We need to resist the notion that dialectical and liberal are mutually exclusive terms. Bultmann reflected on this in an autobiographical piece written at the end of his career:

> It seemed to me that in this new theological movement [i.e., dialectical theology], as distinguished from the "liberal" theology out of which I had come, it was rightly recognized that the Christian faith is not a phenomenon of the history of religion, . . . that therefore theology does not have to look upon Christian faith as a phenomenon of religious or cultural history. It seemed to me that, distinguished from such a view, the new theology correctly saw that Christian faith is the answer to the Word of the transcendent God which encounters the human person, and that theology has to deal with this Word and the person who has been encountered by it. This judgment, however, has never led me to a simple condemnation of "liberal" theology;

41. McCormack, *Karl Barth's Critically Realistic Dialectical Theology*, 264n90.

on the contrary I have endeavored throughout my entire work to carry further the tradition of historical-critical research as it was practiced in "liberal" theology and to make our recent theological knowledge the more fruitful as a result.[42]

QUESTIONS FOR REFLECTION

1. What does it mean to talk *at the same time* of God and ourselves, and how does this differ from more traditional approaches to theology?

2. Is it genuinely possible to speak of a transcendent divine reality that is not simply talk of a "big Other," and if so, how?

3. What similarities are there, if any, between Bultmann's concept of DT and earlier philosophical versions of dialectical thought (e.g., Plato, Hegel, or Kierkegaard)?

4. How might systematic theology look different if we take the existential character of theology seriously as the basis on which to engage in responsible talk of God?

---

42. Bultmann, "Autobiographical Reflections," xxiv.

3

NONOBJECTIFIABILITY

THE TOPIC OF GOD's transcendence or wholly otherness is a key element in Bultmann's understanding of God, but it is only the entry into a more fundamental aspect of his theology, what we might call the doctrine of God's *nonobjectifiability*. In a way, this is the core doctrine of Bultmann's entire theological and hermeneutical program. Clarifying this doctrine will provide us with an interpretive key to the other aspects of his thought. It will also go a long way towards freeing Bultmann from certain entrenched misunderstandings. For instance, as we will see, Bultmann does not set divine transcendence over against immanence as such, but rather against the immanent *in its capacity to be made an object of human reason and use*.

As with most of Bultmann's theological concepts, the idea of nonobjectifiability draws from multiple sources. The four central influences in this case, besides dialectical theology, are New Testament exegesis, Lutheran theology, Marburg Neokantianism, and Heideggerian existentialism. We will look at each of these briefly in turn.

PAULINE *SARX*

Bultmann is always first and foremost a biblical exegete. His theology is essentially *New Testament* theology, specifically in a Pauline and Johannine mold, and at the heart of this theology is an understanding of *sin* and *salvation* as the problem and solution within which the human drama unfolds. In both the NT and Bultmann, the two theological concepts—like the twin foci of an ellipse—imply each other, so to understand one is to understand the other. It therefore does not strictly matter where we begin, so for our purposes here I will focus on the problem of sin. It has to be kept in mind, however, that in doing so I do *not* mean to imply that a prior understanding of sin determines the nature of salvation in Bultmann's theology. On the contrary, as I have argued elsewhere, where it is a question of which aspect is *epistemologically* prior (i.e., which comes first in our knowing), we have to conclude that, for Bultmann, the truth of salvation sets the terms for understanding the truth about sin.[1] We must not think that sin can be known and analyzed—certainly for Bultmann, and arguably for the NT as well—in independence from the event of salvation. Stated in the form of a thesis, we can say: *Salvation may presuppose sin, but the knowledge of sin presupposes the knowledge of salvation*. With this clarification in hand, let us turn now to the biblical, and especially Pauline, depiction of the sinful human condition.

The Pauline account of the human predicament centers around the concept of flesh (σάρξ, *sarx*).[2] Bultmann observes that *sarx* has two different meanings in the NT. Taken in the most straightforward manner, *sarx* carries the

1. See Congdon, *Mission*, 1.2.2.3.

2. The Johannine literature focuses on the concept of world (κόσμος, *kosmos*). This is an equally important term in Bultmann's theology of the NT.

meaning of "material corporeality," though when used syn-ecdochically it can refer to the whole person.[3] But Paul also uses the word in the sense of "fleshliness," meaning "the nature of the earthly-human in its specific humanness—i.e. in its weakness and transitoriness, which also means in op-position to God and His Spirit."[4] Paul thus uses *sarx* as part of his dualistic cosmology, with its binary oppositions be-tween flesh and spirit, visible and invisible, the present evil age and the new creation.[5] It is this latter sense of the term that comes to expression in the adverbial phrase "according to the flesh" (κατὰ σάρκα).

Bultmann notices that Paul uses the phrase "according to the flesh" in two different ways, depending on whether it modifies or refers to a noun (especially persons) or a verb. As an adjectival phrase, "according to the flesh" re-fers to "facts present within natural life and verifiable by everyone."[6] Paul speaks of Christ "was descended from David according to the flesh" (Rom 1:3), of Abraham as our "ancestor according to the flesh" (Rom 4:1), of "my kindred according to the flesh" (Rom 9:3), of "Israel according to the flesh" (1 Cor 10:18, my translation), of "the child who was born according to the flesh" (Gal 4:29; cf. 4:23).[7] In

3. *TNT*, 1:233.

4. Ibid., 1:234.

5. Bultmann observes that Paul does not have a (gnostic) dualism between *body* (or *matter*) and spirit. "Paul conceives the resurrection-life as somatic [i.e., bodily]," and thus he does not reject bodily existence as evil (ibid., 1:199). For Paul, *sarx* represents a "sin-ful power at enmity with God" (ibid., 1:200). When Paul speaks of the need to "put to death the deeds of the body" (Rom 8:13), he is referring to the body "under the sway of *sarx*," that is, enslaved to hostile powers and principalities (ibid.).

6. *TNT*, 1:237.

7. The epistles to the Ephesians and Colossians tell slaves to obey their "masters according to the flesh" (Eph 6:5; Col 3:22, my translation).

each case Paul speaks of things that are natural, earthly, and factual. The contrast to "according to the flesh" is "according to the faith," that is, according to revelation. Instead of "kindred according to the flesh" Paul speaks of those who "belong to Jesus Christ," who are "called to be saints" (Rom 1:6–7). Instead of "Israel according to the flesh," he speaks of the "Israel of God" (Gal 6:16). Instead of the child according to the flesh, he speaks of the "child . . . born through the promise" (Gal 4:23).

As an adverbial phrase, however, "according to the flesh" indicates "*an existence or an attitude* not as natural-human, but *as sinful*."[8] We see this especially in the second letter to the Corinthians, where Paul speaks of "making plans" (2 Cor 1:17), "knowing" (2 Cor 5:16), "walking" (2 Cor 10:2; cf. Rom 8:4), "waging war" (2 Cor 10:3), and "boasting" (2 Cor 11:18) according to the flesh. And in Romans he speaks of "existing" or "being" according to the flesh (Rom 8:5). The contrast in this case is living "according to the Spirit" (Rom 8:4–5), following the axiom of Galatians: "For what the flesh desires is opposed to the Spirit, and what the Spirit desires is opposed to the flesh" (Gal 5:17). Bultmann is quick to point out that the flesh in question here is not something different from the flesh referred to in the adjectival phrases. Doing something "according to the flesh" is sinful because it gives the natural, earthly, factual reality the status of a *norm*.[9] What is visible, objective, and immanent—as opposed to what is invisible, spiritual, and transcendent—is made normative for life and action. The flesh lives according to the past, while the spirit lives according to the future—the future of God revealed in Christ and his Spirit.

8. *TNT*, 1:237.
9. Ibid., 1:238.

If we are looking for the origins of Bultmann's concern for the nonobjectifiability of God, then we need look no further than the NT. To say that God is nonobjectifiable is a way of saying that God cannot be *known according to the flesh.* Paul's statement in 2 Corinthians 5:16 is of central importance. Bultmann finds in this passage the basis for an entire theological epistemology, one that makes revelation, rather than nature, the norm of our thinking, speaking, and doing.[10]

LUTHERAN *SOLA FIDE*

If Bultmann is first and foremost a New Testament theologian, he is secondarily a *Lutheran* theologian. As a biblical scholar, he does not comment specifically on Luther's theology, the way his fellow dialectical theologians Karl Barth and Friedrich Gogarten do. His theology is instead for the most part indirectly and implicitly Lutheran. We will focus on one aspect of Lutheran theology here that bears on Bultmann's concept of divine nonobjectifiability, namely, the doctrine of justification by faith alone (*sola fide*).[11]

The doctrine of justification is crucial to Bultmann's theology on multiple levels. He appeals to the doctrine as the basis for his hermeneutical program, and his discussion of justification is the centerpiece of his exposition of Paul's theology.[12] The relevance of justification to the question of objectification, however, concerns the issue of what

10. In this way, as in so many others, Bultmann anticipates the work of J. Louis Martyn, who refers to this passage as indicative of an "epistemology at the turn of the ages." See Martyn, "Epistemology," 89–110.

11. An equally important heritage of Lutheran theology is the rejection of speculative theology that attempts to speak about God's being in Godself, which Luther called the "hidden God" (*deus absconditus*).

12. See Bultmann, "On the Problem," 122; *TNT*, 1:270–87.

Lutheran theology *opposes* in its emphasis on "faith alone." When Paul speaks of faith in contrast to the "works of the law" (Gal 2:16), or when Luther speaks of faith in contrast to the penitential works of the church, the question is commonly asked whether faith has not simply become a new work, a new means of achieving salvation by one's own effort. Bultmann, following Paul, frequently speaks of faith as a free act of obedience (Rom 1:5, 16:26), which leads him to ask: "If faith is act, does it not follow that we wish to be saved by our own act? If faith is decision, does not our salvation depend on our own resolve?"[13] Luther's response to this question is to say that "faith is not properly referred to as our work . . . but now and then as a kind of work of God."[14] Whereas work corresponds to the law, faith corresponds to the promise. But of course faith is still a willed human activity and experience; the Spirit of God does not operate in us the way a puppeteer controls a marionette.

In order to make sense of faith as both human and divine, Bultmann draws an important distinction between deed or act (*Tat*) and work (*Werk*):

> *Faith* is thus obedience. That is true, of course, but does this not make it a work? It does not, but faith is nevertheless *a deed*. The distinction between work and deed becomes clear when the historical character of human existence is kept firmly in mind. Work, of course, results from a person's doing something; the person is concerned with something objectively present. But the deed is there only in the doing, is never "objectively present." When viewed as external event, as something objectively present, the deed is not seen as a deed.[15]

13. Bultmann, "On the Question," 133.

14. *LW*, 34:160.

15. Bultmann, *What Is Theology?*, 133, rev. The term "objectively

The concept of work refers to something that has an objectifiable effect: for example, it earns wages or gains another's favor. A work achieves something tangible and objective that one can claim for oneself beyond the doing of the work. A deed, by contrast, is not something objectifiable; it cannot be possessed and analyzed as something that exists apart from the acting itself. Bultmann thus refers to faith as a "historical deed," since history, as he understands it, is not something one can observe from an Olympian height. We can only speak about history as an active and responsible participant within it. History is always something *happening*, not an external thing that has *happened*. Christian existence is historical, according to Bultmann, because it is "always present in the here and now, defined by future and past." The believer is constantly being "wakened to life through the claim of the future," and this ever new awakening is the reality of faith, which means "I do not have faith as a possession, as a mental state, as a spiritual quality such as peace of soul or strength of character."[16] Faith is a historical deed in the sense that it has no stable, enduring existence outside of the historical moment. For this reason, Bultmann writes, we can say that "the deed of faith is *worked in us by the Holy Spirit*," in the sense that the Spirit is the effective power, the "how," of the particular moment.[17] Even though it occurs as a human act, faith is an act that we properly attribute to the power of God rather than to our own capacity. Faith is the "work of God," in the words of Luther, precisely *as* a person's act within history. The simultaneous occurrence of divine and human action is what Bultmann identifies by using the word "deed."

---

present" translates the German *vorhanden*, which I discuss below; it is more commonly translated "at hand."

16. Ibid., 138.

17. Ibid., 142.

The foregoing account of faith leads Bultmann to align himself explicitly with the traditional Lutheran account of justification as a *forensic* act. The word "forensic," coming from the Latin word for a public forum, refers to the court of law. A forensic account of justification understands the act in which we are made right before God in terms of a legal declaration of acquittal. The Protestant Reformers argued for the forensic account of justification over against the transformative or ontological account of justification advocated by the Roman Church. By "transformative" or "ontological" we mean that justification according to Rome involved a change in a person's *being*, rather than merely a judicial declaration. The Council of Trent was convened between 1545 and 1563 in response to the Protestant Reformation, and in the sixth session of January 1547 the bishops delivered their decrees regarding justification, which they said "is not only a remission of sins but also the sanctification and renewal of the inward man," whereby "we are truly called and are just, receiving justice within us, . . . which the Holy Ghost distributes to everyone as He wills, and according to each one's disposition and cooperation." This distribution of grace means that, along with the forgiveness of sin, the virtues of faith, hope, and love are "infused at the same time."[18]

Against the Catholic doctrine of infused righteousness (i.e., infused grace), the Reformers propounded their doctrine of *imputed* righteousness. The doctrine of divine imputation—drawn from Paul's claim that "faith was reckoned to Abraham as righteousness" (Rom 4:9; cf. Phil 3:9)—means that, as Luther stated in his 1535 commentary on Galatians, "God overlooks these sins, and in His sight they are as though they were not sins. This is accomplished by imputation on account of the faith by which I begin to

18. Schroeder, *Canons*, 33–34.

39

take hold of Christ; and on His account God reckons imperfect righteousness as perfect righteousness and sin as not sin, even though it really is sin."[19] Luther argued for imputed righteousness in contrast to the Catholic "sophists" who "suppose that righteousness is a certain quality that is first infused into the soul and then distributed through all the members."[20] Luther and his followers denied that sanctification and renewal belong in the article on justification not because good works are unimportant but because "they are never fully pure and perfect in this life," and to make justification contingent on moral transformation would undermine the "reliable and certain comfort" promised in the gospel. For this reason justifying faith "relies neither on contrition nor on love or other virtues, but only on Christ."[21] Our righteousness, therefore, "is not in us . . . but is outside us, solely in the grace of God and in His imputation."[22] Imputed righteousness is *alien* righteousness, meaning that it is wholly outside of us, and it is "outside" in the sense that our perfect righteousness remains wholly *eschatological*, entirely *future*, as indicated by the above statement that we are "never fully pure and perfect in this life." Within the present moment, the believer is both in history and therefore a sinner and beyond history and thus perfectly righteous. For this reason, in Luther's famous words, the Christian "is righteous and a sinner at the same time, holy and profane, an enemy of God and a child of God. None of the sophists will admit this paradox, because they do not understand the true meaning of justification."[23]

19. *LW*, 26:232.

20. *LW*, 26:233.

21. Formula of Concord, Solid Declaration, Article III, in Kolb and Wengert, *Book of Concord*, 566–67 (§§28, 30).

22. *LW*, 26:234.

23. *LW*, 26:232–33.

Bultmann finds the traditional Lutheran account of justification compelling because it captures doctrinally the distinction within the New Testament between eschatology and history, between transcendence and immanence, between flesh and spirit, between God and the world. In his lectures on theology Bultmann indicates his agreement with this position by citing several Lutheran authorities. He quotes a passage from the Apology of the Augsburg Confession that defines justification as a forensic act in which a person is pronounced righteous on the basis of an "*alien* righteousness."[24] More surprisingly, he cites Lutheran scholastic theologians, including Johann Wilhelm Baier, David Hollaz, and Johannes Andreas Quenstedt. He quotes Hollaz as saying that because justification "takes place *outside* the human person in God, it cannot intrinsically change the person."[25] In accord with Lutheran theology, Bultmann claims that "forgiveness . . . is not an objectively present something that is at some time or other at one's disposal."[26] Bultmann gives the example of a historical fact, like the crossing of the Rubicon, which is accessible to anyone and can be treated like any other object of knowledge. If justification were like that, then it would "divide life into two halves," namely, into life before and after justification. Righteousness would be the possession of the believer, in the same way that knowledge about the past is the possession of the historian. Such a view, however, would turn faith into a work and thereby undermine our confidence in God's forgiveness of sin. It would also violate the historical nature of human existence. Either our righteousness is within us as something infusable, acquirable, and objectifiable, or our righteousness is outside of us in Christ alone—and thus ac-

24. Bultmann, *What Is Theology?*, 139, rev.
25. Ibid., rev.
26. Ibid., rev.

cessible by faith alone—in which case we can be assured of its efficacy and reality. The former locates security in the flesh, while the latter locates it in the Spirit. The former seeks security in what can be grasped and possessed, which turns out to be fleeting and ultimately full of despair; the latter abandons all security in oneself only to discover genuine security in what cannot be grasped or objectified.

Given the way Bultmann's theology is consistently grounded in soteriology, his talk of objectification almost always has this polarity between faith and works in view, even when he is not specifically discussing the doctrine of justification. He occasionally makes the connection explicit, as in his 1952 defense of his program of demythologizing, in the conclusion to which he says that "radical demythologizing is the parallel to the Pauline-Lutheran doctrine of justification through faith alone without the works of the law. Or, rather, it is the consistent application of this doctrine to the field of knowledge. Like the doctrine of justification, it destroys every false security and every false demand for security, whether it is grounded on our good action or on our certain knowledge."[27] Earlier in that same essay he defines myth as "an objectifying kind of thinking" and states that demythologizing "seeks to bring out the real intention of myth, namely, its intention to talk about human existence as grounded in and limited by a transcendent, unworldly power, which is not visible to objectifying thinking."[28] We do not need to discuss the topic of myth here (see chapter 7). It is enough to observe that the relationship between myth and demythologizing corresponds to the relationship between works and faith. The claim that our knowledge of God depends on the literal infallibility of biblical mythology is the epistemological equivalent to the claim that our

27. Bultmann, "On the Problem," 122.
28. Ibid., 98–99.

justification by God depends on the inner experience and transformation of the individual. In both cases our security—whether epistemological (knowledge) or soteriological (justification)—is located in something objectifiable, such as the biblical text or the individual person. As a Lutheran theologian, Bultmann rejects the soteriological form of objectification, and in a sense his project is nothing more than the consistent extension of the *sola fide* to every other area of Christian thought.

NEOKANTIAN *OBJEKTIVIERUNG*

As a student at the University of Marburg, Bultmann came into contact with the Marburg school of Neokantianism, represented by Hermann Cohen and Paul Natorp. Bultmann would have learned about this school of thought when he studied Kant in 1906 under Natorp. Neokantianism arose as a way of correcting Kant's epistemology in light of the criticisms of Hegel and his followers. In essence, the correction involved removing the gap between subject and object. Whereas Kant understood the object of thought to be an empirical reality perceived through sense experience, the Neokantians understood the object to be the product of thought, in strict accordance with the laws of logic. The subject of this thinking is not the individual human person, as in Kant, but instead, like Hegel, "the subject means spirit [*Geist*]."[29] The process by which spirit produces the object of thought is called "objectification" (*Objektivierung*). According to Natorp, "every presentation of an object . . . is an objectification."[30]

The point is that talk of objectification signifies for Bultmann a process whereby scientific reason constructs

29. Cohen, *Logik*, 218.
30. Natorp, *Allgemeine Psychologie*, 42.

and comprehends the world. Marburg Neokantianism elevates reason and logic into the all-encompassing principles that determine meaning. This is why Bultmann often refers to "objectifying thinking." It is the *thinking* aspect of objectification, specifically the way it makes human rationality into the norm for all truth claims, that he wants to highlight as particularly problematic. Cohen exemplifies the problem when he places logic, reason, and science over against religion and myth, which he associates with animal instinct.[31] Human rationality and scientific logic are effectively the principles that govern the world. From Bultmann's perspective, the Neokantian emphasis on objectifying thinking is the idolization of the human spirit.

While Bultmann's understanding of objectification and objectifying thinking is not limited to Neokantianism, it is a decisive factor shaping his appropriation and use of these terms. By pursuing a theology without objectification, Bultmann is pursuing an epistemology that does not reduce all objects of knowledge to what scientific reason is able to posit or comprehend. A God who is genuinely transcendent is not at the disposal of human thought. Such a God is therefore nonobjectifiable.

HEIDEGGERIAN *VORHANDENHEIT*

The fourth source for Bultmann's understanding of objectifying thinking is Martin Heidegger's philosophy and specifically his concept of *Vorhandenheit* (or *Vorhandensein*), translated variously as presence-at-hand or objective presence, a term we have seen already in Bultmann's work. Heidegger develops this idea in his seminal work, *Being and Time*, where he makes a distinction between two terms: *existentia* and *Existenz*. He defines *existentia* as *Vorhandenheit*,

31. Cohen, *Logik*, 364–66.

which refers, he says, to an entity in its "outward appearance," entities such as a table, a human body, or a utensil.[32] The objective presence of an entity consists in its capacity to be "*observed* and stared at simply as something present."[33]

Heidegger differentiates the objective presence associated with *existentia* from the concept of existence (*Existenz*). He associates the latter with what he calls *Dasein*,[34] which is the distinct existence that characterizes the being of the human person—a being distinguished from other creatures or objects by the fact that it is *concerned* about its own being. *Dasein* is defined by what Heidegger calls "being-in-the-world," but "we cannot understand by this the objective presence of a material thing." The "in" in "being-*in*-the-world" is not like water being "in" the glass.[35] Objective presence is "essentially inappropriate to characterize the being which has the character of Dasein," since the characteristics of *Dasein* are not observable attributes.[36] Whereas objective presence refers to the "whatness" (*Was-sein*) of something, *Dasein* refers to

32. Heidegger, *Being and Time*, 41.

33. Ibid., 73. Heidegger argues that an object's character of being present and available for empirical observation is fundamentally secondary to its "handiness" (*Zuhandenheit*), that is to say, its familiarity as something ready to be used by someone for a particular task. This handiness is prereflective, meaning that we regularly and habitually use objects without consciously reflecting on the object itself in its objective presence. So a hammer is ready to be used for the task of hitting a nail, and we use it for this purpose without examining the *existentia* or presence of the hammer itself.

34. The word literally means "being-there" (*Da* means "there" and *Sein* means "being"). The word is generally used in German as the equivalent of the English word "existence," but Heidegger makes a conceptual distinction between *Dasein* and *Existenz*. Many translations of Heidegger and Bultmann leave *Dasein* untranslated to avoid confusion.

35. Heidegger, *Being and Time*, 50.

36. Ibid., 41.

"being" (*Sein*).[37] This distinctively human "being" does not manifest itself as part of the world of empirical objects, but rather it becomes "visible as *care*,"[38] that is, as *concern* for the existence of others. Heidegger's language can be confusing but his point is simple: human existence cannot be reduced to the status of something objectively present that can be observed and used.

This is, of course, only a cursory glance at some of Heidegger's key concepts, but a cursory glance is all we need. Bultmann's project does not depend on Heidegger's ontology. Bultmann develops his early account of God's nonobjectifiability before ever encountering Heidegger's work, and there is evidence to suggest that Heidegger was at least as influenced by Bultmann as the other way around. Nevertheless, subsequent to his encounter with Heidegger's work in *Being and Time*, we see Bultmann begin to appropriate certain philosophical concepts. One of the most important is *Vorhandenheit* (or simply the adjective *vorhanden*). As we have seen, Bultmann uses this concept as a technical theological term to describe an understanding of divine action that makes it accessible to any person apart from faith. In other words, to view God as *vorhanden* is to objectify God.

Several passages from his posthumously published lectures on theology, originally given between 1926 and 1936, will show how he puts this idea to use. He says that the attempt to find God's revelation outside of the Christ known to faith alone "makes the revelation something objectively present [*Vorhandenen*], human. If it is a claim made upon me, then it can never be confirmed as something objectively present."[39] He elsewhere says that "forgive-

37. Ibid., 41–42.
38. Ibid., 57.
39. Bultmann, *What Is Theology?*, 90, rev.

ness is, of course, not a fact to be documented, something objectively present."[40] Bultmann thus uses the concept of objective presence to help differentiate between faith and works. Whereas work is "concerned with something that is objectively present," faith is a deed or act that "is there only in the doing, is never 'objectively present,'" precisely because it is faith in the God who is not objectively present.[41] Faith is correspondingly absent when we "cling to the visible, to what is objectively present, instead of to the invisible."[42] Bultmann associates objective presence not only with works of the law, but also with death, the past, and the flesh.[43] Sin occurs when one places trust in what is present-at-hand, when one makes what is objectively present into the norm for one's thinking and doing. Living "according to the Spirit," by contrast, occurs when one does *not* cling to what is objectively present:

> If σάρξ [flesh] is the sphere of the world of what is objectively present and designates a conduct κατὰ σάρκα [according to the flesh], an understanding and securing of one's self on the basis of what is objectively present, then the πνεῦμα [spirit] means what is not objectively present and a conduct κατὰ πνεῦμα [according to the Spirit] means a life which loses itself—for nothing, from the standpoint of the world—in order to live from the future.[44]

If it is not already evident, it should be noted that Bultmann does not use *Vorhandenheit* in the precise way that Heidegger uses the concept within his fundamental

40. Ibid., 102, rev.
41. Ibid., 133, rev.
42. Ibid., 147, rev.
43. See ibid., 138, 143.
44. Bultmann, "Christology," 275, rev.

ontology. Bultmann retains the association of *Vorhanden-heit* with what is visible and observable, but he means visibility in a metaphorical (i.e., theological) rather than strictly literal sense, in the same way that Paul uses *sarx* metaphorically in the phrase "according to the flesh." Bultmann uses *Vorhandenheit* as a synonym for *sarx*: "to know others from the standpoint that they are flesh [means] to know them in their pure, general, visible objective presence."[45] "According to the flesh" is here identical to "according to what is objectively present." Of course, the point is not that the sinner actually determines her life on the basis of inanimate objects in the world. Bultmann instead means that the sinner lives as if she has control over her own existence, as if she were not dependent upon a transcendent power and authority. In this light, it becomes clear that the biblical-theological notions of spirit and flesh, faith and works, are the criteria for Bultmann's appropriation of Heidegger and Neokantianism. Bultmann constricts philosophy within the space determined by the biblical text.

GOD IS NOT A GIVEN ENTITY

How then does this composite notion of objectifiability manifest itself in Bultmann's theological writings? Shortly after his turn to dialectical theology, Bultmann gave several blistering lectures against liberal theology, in which he accused the liberal theologians of objectifying God. These theologians, he says, try "to view God as a given entity [*Gegebenheit*], as an object of the kind to which the relationship of direct knowledge is possible for us."[46] By "direct knowledge" he means the kind of knowledge one has of the observable world, the kind thematized by both the

45. Bultmann, "Church and Teaching," 217, rev.
46. Bultmann, "Liberal Theology," 33.

Neokantians and Heidegger. Against this he argues: "*God is not a given entity.* . . . God's revelation does not make God something known in the sense of rational knowledge [*Vernunfterkennens*]."[47] The reference here to reason (*Vernunft*) is almost certainly an allusion to Neokantianism. The liberal attempt to reconstruct religion within the bounds of reason—for example, by reconstructing Jesus according to historical research—is an attempt, in fact, to make God "an object of thought."[48]

Many years later Bultmann commented on the christological confession of the World Council of Churches. He criticized the ancient creedal formulas for the "objectifying nature" of the Greek metaphysics used to articulate the fact that Jesus Christ is the eschatological event.[49] This event can neither "be objectified into an event of the past, nor into an event in a metaphysical sphere. . . . The formula 'Christ is God' is false in every sense in which God is understood as an objectifiable entity, whether it is understood in an Arian or Nicene, an Orthodox or a Liberal sense."[50] Both orthodox and liberal theologies are subject to critique by Bultmann for the way they talk about God as an observable object. The problem in both cases is the use of what is immanent and worldly as a norm for understanding God. Orthodoxy uses ancient philosophy, while liberalism uses historical research. Either way results in a knowledge of God "according to the flesh," that is, a knowledge through works rather than by faith.

The solution for Bultmann is twofold. First, we cannot speak about what God is in Godself—that is to say, about God's nature or being—but only of what God *does.*

47. Ibid., 45, rev.
48. Bultmann, "What Does It Mean," 53.
49. Bultmann, "Christological Confession," 286, rev.
50. Ibid., 287, rev.

Bultmann takes this idea from Wilhelm Herrmann (though it derives ultimately from Luther and Melanchthon), whom he quotes as saying: "Of God we can only tell what [God] does to us."[51] This axiom methodologically and materially restricts talk of God to what we encounter in revelation, which for Bultmann occurs in Jesus Christ, who meets us here and now in the proclamation of God's word. But the question remains how to understand the relation between this human word of proclamation and the reality of God. This leads to the second part of Bultmann's solution: the concept of paradox or paradoxical identity. Orthodoxy and liberalism both assume a *direct* identity between something in the world and God, whether this is a miraculous occurrence or a historical fact. Apophatic theologies posit a *nonidentity* between God and the world,[52] which precludes the possibility of genuine knowledge and talk of God—something Bultmann refuses to abandon. The alternative is a *paradoxical* identity, which argues that God acts in history, but in a way that is accessible only to faith.[53] Theology without objectification thus speaks of God's revelatory action in history as an event that truly happens but that never becomes an observable part of the world. It is an event that

51. Bultmann, "What Does It Mean," 63.

52. Apophatic (or negative) theology refers to a mode of speaking about God in which one can only say what God is *not*. For example, it is apophatic to say that God is "infinite" (not-finite) or "immortal" (not-mortal). Apophatic theology posits a strong separation between God and creation but denies any positive relationship between them, since that would allow us to say what God *is*. God stands utterly beyond the world. Obviously, this presents difficulties for christology. It also largely *assumes* we cannot say what God is rather than proves it, which raises the question whether the limits of God-talk are being determined by what *we* think is possible, rather than what is actually possible for God.

53. See Bultmann, *Jesus Christ*, 62.

must happen again and again, which we can never prove but can only proclaim anew.

QUESTIONS FOR REFLECTION

1. Bultmann focuses on Protestant orthodoxy and liberalism as instances of the objectification of God. What are some other ways that Christians objectify God, whether in theology, the church, or society? What would have to change if we confessed a nonobjectifiable God?

2. Bultmann was himself critical of the recitation of the ancient creeds as part of the church's liturgy. Is there more to the creeds than objectifying thinking? Is there a way of incorporating the creeds that is not inherently a form of objectification?

3. What does a nonobjectifiable understanding of God mean for belief in miracles? How might we conceive of miracles in a nonobjectifiable way?

4. Is there a way to speak meaningfully of God's *being* that does not objectify God?

4

SELF-UNDERSTANDING

FAITH, AS WE HAVE seen, is at the heart of Bultmann's theological project. Apart from faith we are unable to know or speak about God. But what exactly does Bultmann mean by "faith"? Here we arrive at one of his most contested ideas— the notion that faith is "self-understanding" (*Selbstverständnis*). Karl Barth's criticisms of this idea are representative. In his *Church Dogmatics*, he speaks of the "sphere of self-understanding," as if self-understanding identifies a field of knowledge whose propositions are *derived from the self*. So he asks: "Within the sphere of self-understanding how can he ever come . . . to confess that he is finally and totally guilty in relation to God and his neighbour and himself?"[1] The "act of self-understanding" posits an "imaginary god" that is "simply a reflection of our own existence" and a "mythologized" version of "our conversation with ourselves."[2] Finally, Barth claims, "if we start with ourselves we can never say the things which have to be said."[3]

1. *CD* 4.1:360.
2. *CD* 4.1:364–65, rev.
3. *CD* 4.1:479.

Statements like these have been made by many theologians over the years—and for understandable reasons. The term "self-understanding" certainly *sounds* suspicious. And if theologians as bright and knowledgeable as Barth interpret Bultmann's language this way, it is no wonder that others do so as well. Many of the controversies and misunderstandings surrounding Bultmann's theology rest on terminological issues like this. People assume that "demythologizing" is not only anti-myth but an attempt to extract a kerygma free from mythology. People assume that "existentialist interpretation" must be an interpretation determined by existentialist philosophy. These and other assumptions quickly prove false upon examination, but the instinctive reaction against the terms themselves often prevents people from bothering to examine any further.

TWO KINDS OF SELF-UNDERSTANDING

A brief exploration of Bultmann's concept of self-understanding reveals that, fairly early on in his career, he describes two different kinds of self-understanding. He sets this out most clearly in his 1929 essay on "Church and Teaching in the New Testament." As with many of his essays, he begins by describing a position that he will later criticize or modify by appealing to the NT. In this case the question is what it means to speak of "teaching" (*Lehre*). What does it mean, in other words, to communicate knowledge about the world, and how does this relate to teaching within the church?

Bultmann starts by distinguishing between two modes of communicating knowledge. The first is the communication "of *facts which I cannot know of myself*," that is, facts about historical occurrences or objects in the world.[4]

4. Bultmann, "Church and Teaching," 185. Future citations in parentheses.

The second is the "knowledge of principles" regarding the world that I already know implicitly but which the teaching makes explicit (186). These include mathematical laws (e.g., the commutative law), scientific theories (e.g., the theory of gravity), laws of logic (e.g., the law of noncontradiction), and other supposedly timeless truths. These two modes of teaching "form a *unity*," since facts always include principles and principles are always related to facts; "communication of the one kind always results in communication of the other" (186). What also unifies both forms of knowledge is that neither "tell[s] me anything that is *new in a fundamental sense*" (186). Both facts and principles are things that people can find out for themselves, if they just put in the necessary work. In each case the knowledge in question concerns "the world that I already know in principle" (186). And since "all understanding of anything (that is, of anything in the world) is always ultimately an understanding of myself, a 'finding my own place in my world,'" it follows that these two forms of knowledge concern an understanding of the self that I already know in principle (187):

> In all such factual knowledge or knowledge of principles, the world is presumed to have the character of something objectively present [*Vorhandenen*], passive, accessible to simple observation. . . . In such a conception of the world as an objectively present entity [*vorhandener*], human beings are regarded as objectively present (as a fragment of the cosmos); their self-understanding [*Sich-verstehen*] is achieved along with the understanding of the world (and vice versa). That is, it is assumed that they have themselves fundamentally under their own control and completely under observation ("know thyself," γνῶθι σαυτόν); they can learn to understand themselves better and better, but

> not in any basically new way. Their original
> self-understanding [*Sichverstehen*] can merely
> become explicit. (187, rev.)

Bultmann here makes a direct connection between Heideggerian objective presence and a certain mode of self-understanding. When I understand the world as present-at-hand, as scientifically analyzable, and so under my control, I also understand myself in the same way. This form of knowledge is, as we examined in the previous chapter, a knowledge "according to the flesh."

In contrast to this rational and scientific self-understanding, rooted in a rational and scientific understanding of the world—and which he associates with ancient Greek thought—there is what we might call an existential or historical self-understanding. This alternative understanding is premised on the assumption that "something new can be known," which is only possible if human existence "does not have the character of something objectively present, but rather has the character of *historical* [*geschichtlich*] being" (187, rev.). Historical self-understanding is possible where it is recognized that one "can *become* a new person" and so can understand oneself in a fundamentally new way (187). This new self-understanding is historical in the sense that it is a response to a particular event or encounter within a historical situation here and now, which "cannot possibly be 'seen' . . . as an objective fact," but "can only be heard as a summons" (187). For this reason, one's historical self-understanding "never has the character of a knowledge of something objectively present [*Vorhandenes*], and therefore self-understanding itself does not have the character of being objectively present [*Vorhandenheit*], but is seized only in resolve" (188, rev.). In other words, one has to understand oneself anew each time.

This much describes existential or historical self-understanding in general. There is nothing particularly *Christian* about this account. The summons in question could be the claim of, among other things, a lover, a parent, a child, or even a political cause. "Such examples do not, however, fully define the content of the church's kerygma," which communicates not only new possibilities of existence but also facts—specifically, "*eschatological* facts" that describe "divine acts, . . . events in a history of salvation," which are "incomprehensible on the basis of a given understanding of the world" and "undiscoverable by any investigation of the world" (189). The self-understanding communicated in the church's kerygma thus places my very self at risk. My entire existence is at stake. To be confronted by the kerygma is to be faced with a reality in which "I do not have the freedom to refuse to choose and so to remain my old self" (192). This reality, which Paul describes as participating in the risen life of Jesus, "is not world history . . . but is eschatological event," and thus being "in Christ" and a "new creation" means "to stand within this new history" and "to belong to the new world" (202).

THE STRANGE NEW WORLD OF FAITH

We are now in a position to see that, when Bultmann calls faith a new self-understanding, this has nothing to do with a knowledge *about* oneself, as if faith were the communication of new information about one's existence. Nor does it mean that faith is generated out of some latent potential in our natural human existence. For those who share Barth's view, self-understanding can be contrasted with an understanding of God as revealed in Christ through the witness of scripture. It does not matter much whether the self stands in place of the "God revealed in Christ" as the content of understanding or in the place of scripture as the medium of this understanding. We are left either with an understanding that lacks God or a natural theology that lacks a revelation from outside ourselves.

Bultmann's actual position is quite different. The individual human person is neither the content nor the source of revelation, but rather the *site*. It is where revelation *occurs as revelation*. And that is because what the church "teaches" in its proclamation is not factual or general information about the empirical (i.e., objectively present) world that has nothing to do with my life or that I could learn on my own. It is instead a message about a strange new world, the eschatological world of new creation, and this message is inherently self-involving. To hear the message is already to be claimed by it. We either obey this claim or we do not. Indeed, its claim upon us is precisely the content of revelation: "Its content is thus neither nature nor a history of which one may be aware, since there is no knowledge of it. It is not perceptible as world. It is not a *ginōskein*, but a *gnōsthēnai* (Gal. 4:9; 1 Cor. 8:2f.; 13:12)."[5] Faith is not *choosing* or *knowing* God, but rather *acknowledging* that we are *known by God* and living obediently in accordance with that acknowledgment. Bultmann calls this "radical obedience," because in this obedience one's "own real being is at stake—that self which one not already is, but is to become."[6] Faith is an act of surrender to the claim of God, in which, paradoxically, one ends up gaining oneself (cf. Luke 17.33). Gaining oneself by submitting to God—*this* is what Bultmann means by self-understanding.

Bultmann presents this account of faith in the "Church and Teaching" essay referenced above, where he writes:

5. Bultmann, *What Is Theology?*, 84.
6. *TNT*, 1:15.

The Word is understood only . . . in the obedience of faith. Therefore, the proclamation is not a mere factual communication which could be given once for all. It is preached again and again, continually. For in the communication of the fact of salvation there is a summons, a question to be decided, an invitation. "Now we are ambassadors for Christ, as though God did beseech you by us; we pray you in Christ's stead, be ye reconciled to God" (II Cor. 5.20). . . . *Understanding* does not mean the ability to deduce from [the proclamation] an explanation for fitting what is proclaimed into the previously held world picture. That is exactly what *cannot* be done. The proclamation is a "stumbling-block" and "folly"; but "so it pleased God" (I Cor. 1.21). *Understanding* means rather that under the impact of hearing the proclamation, the individual has learned to understand oneself anew, to understand oneself as the sinner to whom God is giving justification. (209, rev.)

Christian self-understanding cannot be derived from or fit into our previous understanding of the world (i.e., our previous self-understanding). It is a scandalous word that calls a person into question and proclaims a message of gracious justification to the sinner. As a message of grace, the very possibility of hearing and responding to this word depends on "the operation of the divine act," which is an "event that puts the human person in a new situation" (210, rev.). Contrary to his critics, Bultmann's concept of self-understanding actually means that one looks *away* from oneself in order to find oneself. "If one looks only at oneself one's past is 'flesh,' is sin and death," but revelation proclaims a forgiveness that frees one "for a future determined by the promise" (200–201, rev.).

We can therefore define Bultmann's concept of theological self-understanding as follows: *Self-understanding is the event in which a person encounters the word of God and so discovers herself to be a sinner who has received justification by God's grace, and who has therefore been given a new future, a new life, a new world.* Faith as self-understanding has nothing to do with a solipsistic turning inward upon oneself. It rather means *being placed outside ourselves* and into a new historical existence, and thus it is the "exact opposite of a dwelling-on-oneself."[7] For Bultmann, following Paul (cf. Gal 3:23), faith is the advent of new creation: "Could faith then be the Archimedean point from which the world is moved off its axis and is transformed from the world of sin into the world of God? Yes! That is the message of faith."[8]

In his introduction to the English translation of *Faith and Understanding*, Robert Funk states: "Only a consistent misreading of Bultmann could have led to the sort of 'subjectivistic' interpretation of Bultmann's term 'self-understanding' found in many of Bultmann's critics. . . . In order to correct the misunderstanding precipitated by the term 'self-understanding,' it may prove necessary to replace that term by the term 'world.'"[9] Funk wrote these words nearly thirty years ago, but they remain just as relevant today.

7. Jüngel, "Glauben," 61.

8. Bultmann, "What Does It Mean," 64.

9. Funk, introduction to *Faith and Understanding*, 25–26. Cf. Bultmann's clarification of self-understanding in his 1952 essay on demythologizing: "Is it really so hard to understand what is meant by 'existential self-understanding'? In any case, there is nothing but complete lack of understanding behind the objection that by this designation the event of revelation is degraded to the occasion that releases self-understanding and therefore is no longer acknowledged as a fact that intervenes in reality and transforms it, and thus as a wonder" (Bultmann, "On the Program," 115).

"THESE TWO THINGS BELONG TOGETHER, FAITH AND GOD"

As I noted in a previous chapter, one of the frequent charges brought against Bultmann's theology is that he reduces theology to anthropology, and his concept of faith as self-understanding is often cited as Exhibit A for this reduction. We have already seen that the existential character of DT ensures that we are speaking of the transcendent God and not a pseudo-god. Theology is *dialectical* in order to prevent the objectification of God. For Bultmann, faith is *self-understanding* for precisely the same reason. Faith understands God only by simultaneously understanding oneself, because the God I encounter in revelation is the God who justifies me. Knowledge of God on different terms would be knowledge of a different object, a knowledge of God "according to the flesh," that is, a knowledge of God as an objectively present entity under my rational control. To prevent the scientific domestication of God, the knowledge of faith "is understanding *as* the *self-understanding* in which one comprehends the Revealer and one's self."[10] We either comprehend both at the same time, or we comprehend neither.

In all of this Bultmann is simply being a good Lutheran theologian. His entire account of theology as existential, of God as nonobjectifiable, and of faith as self-understanding can be understood as the consistent elaboration of Luther's statement in his Large Catechism that "these two things belong together, faith and God."[11]

10. Bultmann, "Eschatology," 183.

11. Luther, "Large Catechism," 386. There is also another aspect to this: Bultmann spent some of the most decisive years of his career (1933–45) resisting the Nazi regime. He lived within a totalitarian political culture that demanded each person sacrifice his or her individuality to the cause of the nation. His emphasis on decision and

QUESTIONS FOR REFLECTION

1. What connotations does the term "self-understanding" evoke for you? Are they positive or negative? Why do you think that is the case?

2. What self-understandings are promoted and rewarded within your social, cultural, political, and ecclesial contexts? How are these similar to or different from Christian self-understanding?

3. What might it mean for faith to be the entrance into a "new world" or a "new history"?

4. In what ways does current church practice hinder or foster the discovery of a new self-understanding?

---

the self was a countercultural way of recognizing and affirming each person's moral responsibility. He gave people the theological space to see themselves in the light of God's word, rather than in the light of "blood and soil." Within a North American context, such talk can sound like Bultmann is giving theological support to the rampant libertarian individualism that pervades Western society. As always, context matters.

5

KERYGMA

PERHAPS NO TERM IS more closely and immediately associated with Bultmann than "kerygma." But what exactly does it mean? And what is the context for its use? Bultmann and his followers tend to use "kerygma" in place of the more common term "gospel," but there is much more going on here than a mere lexical substitution. We will unpack the concept in this chapter by looking at how Bultmann understands its relation to early Christianity, church proclamation, and contemporary systematic theology.[1]

KERYGMA AS THE PROBLEM OF NEW TESTAMENT THEOLOGY

The word κήρυγμα (*kerugma*, proclamation) appears nine times in the NT—four times in the undisputed letters of Paul.[2] As Bultmann's student Gerhard Ebeling observes,

---

1. For an excellent discussion of the kerygma within Bultmann's New Testament theology, see Kay, *Christus Praesens*, 48–60.

2. The verb κηρύσσειν (*kerussein*, to proclaim) appears over sixty times in various forms, but this is a generic word referring to any act of proclaiming or preaching. The nominal form is more distinctive.

"kerygma is not a central concept of the New Testament."[3] Nevertheless, Bultmann's choice of the term is strategic, since the appearances of κήρυγμα in the NT indicate a connection between proclamation, revelation, and salvation in early Christianity. At the end of Romans, we read: "Now to God who is able to strengthen you according to my gospel and the proclamation [κήρυγμα] of Jesus Christ, according to the revelation of the mystery that was kept secret for long ages but is now disclosed . . ." (Rom 16:25–26a). In the opening of 1 Corinthians, Paul writes: "For since, in the wisdom of God, the world did not know God through wisdom, God decided, through the foolishness of our proclamation, to save those who believe" (1 Cor 1:21). And again: "My speech and my proclamation were not with plausible words of wisdom, but with a demonstration of the Spirit and of power, so that your faith might rest not on human wisdom but on the power of God" (1 Cor 2:4–5). Even more strikingly, Paul says later in the same letter that "if Christ has not been raised, then our proclamation has been in vain and your faith has been in vain" (1 Cor 15:14). In the deutero-Pauline letters, we read that "the Lord was present with me and gave me strength, so that through me the proclamation might be fulfilled and all the Gentiles might hear it" (2 Tim 4:17, my translation), and "in his appointed time he has revealed his word through the proclamation" (Titus 1:3, my translation). It is clear from the NT, therefore, that kerygma or proclamation is the vehicle of God's saving power, the human word through which God's word of revelation confronts us.

But what *is* the kerygma? What is the *content* of this proclamation that Paul says is the means by which God saves those who believe? For Bultmann, the primary task of New Testament interpretation is to answer this question. In

3. Ebeling, "Kerygma," 516.

a letter to Martin Heidegger in December 1932, Bultmann writes: "It is becoming increasingly apparent to me that the central problem of New Testament theology is to say what the Christian kerygma actually is."[4] A key to addressing this problem comes from the close connection in Paul's letters between kerygma and the gospel preached by the early church, readily seen in the passages quoted above. In fact, apart from the two synoptic references to the "proclamation of Jonah" (Matt 12:41; Luke 11:32), every appearance of kerygma in the NT refers to the message of the *church* regarding the revelation of God in Christ—specifically, in Christ crucified and risen, which is the sum and substance of Paul's preaching.[5] Jesus might be the *proclaimer*, but he does not bring the *proclamation*. The kerygma, it would seem, is a distinctively post-Easter message.

In order to answer the question "what the Christian kerygma actually is," Bultmann thus differentiates between "the message [*Verkündigung*] of Jesus" and "the kerygma of the earliest church."[6] He opens his *Theology of the New Testament* with the famous statement:

> *The message of Jesus* is a presupposition for the theology of the New Testament rather than a part of that theology itself. For New Testament theology consists in the unfolding of those ideas by means of which Christian faith makes sure of its own object, basis, and consequences. But

4. Bultmann and Heidegger, *Briefwechsel*, 186.

5. This is perhaps most strikingly illustrated in the Gospel of Mark, where the word only appears in the later addition of Mark 16:8: "And afterward Jesus himself sent out through them, from east to west, the sacred and imperishable proclamation of eternal salvation." This suggests that the word is associated with the official church teaching regarding Christ as the messiah of God. Bultmann uses the word with this precise meaning in mind.

6. *TNT*, 1:3, 33.

> Christian faith did not exist until there was a
> Christian kerygma; i.e., a kerygma proclaiming
> Jesus Christ—specifically Jesus Christ the Cru-
> cified and Risen One—to be God's eschatologi-
> cal act of salvation. He was first so proclaimed
> in the kerygma of the earliest Church, not in the
> message of the historical Jesus.[7]

Christian faith is faith in Jesus crucified and risen, and
therefore the Christian kerygma cannot be the message
preached by Jesus. Whereas Jesus proclaimed the news of
God's reign that is near at hand, the church proclaimed
Jesus as the messiah who is the savior of the world. In Bultmann's words, "he who formerly had been the *bearer* of the
message was drawn into it and became its essential *content.
The proclaimer became the proclaimed.*"[8]

It is this transition from proclaimer to proclaimed
that sets Christianity apart from Judaism.[9] The message
of Jesus, while radical, operated within Israel's prophetic
tradition; it was "only the consummation of tendencies that
underlie the preaching of the great prophets."[10] One could
be a follower of Jesus' teachings and remain within the
Jewish faith. What differentiates Christianity is the claim
that this apocalyptic prophet, crucified by the Romans, was
raised and exalted by God to be the eschatological judge of
the world. The kerygma is therefore the uniquely *Christian*
element within Christianity. What the church proclaims
in the kerygma is neither the personality or consciousness
of Jesus, the historical facts surrounding his life, nor even
the details of his teachings, as the letters of Paul indicate.

7. Ibid., 1:3.

8. Ibid., 1:33.

9. In this early period, Christianity is best understood as a sect
within Judaism in distinction from the developing rabbinic Judaism.

10. *TNT*, 1:34.

Instead, the church proclaims *Jesus himself* as messiah, that is, as the eschatological event. The sheer fact of his having come to the world is itself the kerygma: "Indeed, that is the real content of the Easter faith: God has made the prophet and teacher Jesus of Nazareth Messiah!"[11] And Jesus is revealed as the messiah in the event of his death-and-resurrection.[12] The community of believers then interprets everything else from that perspective: "the kerygma of Jesus as Messiah is the basic and primary thing which gives everything else—the ancient tradition and Jesus' message—its special character."[13]

Walter Schmithals, in his afterword to Bultmann's *Jesus*, summarizes the latter's position as follows: "The gospel, according to Bultmann, is not the preaching of Jesus, but rather the preaching about Jesus as the crucified and risen one. Only as the proclaimed, not as the proclaimer, is the person of Jesus Christ the content of the kerygma."[14] While this accurately presents Bultmann's position regarding early Christianity, what does the kerygma of Jesus as the Christ mean for the community of faith *today*?

KERYGMA AS WORD-EVENT

To say that the content of the kerygma is that Jesus of Nazareth is the messiah can mean a number of different things. For those inclined to see this NT confession as an incipient creed, the claim that Jesus is the messiah is a theological proposition regarding something objectively, perhaps even verifiably, true. It is an assertion of fact, like saying that Jesus was a Jew or that Jesus had disciples. Kerygma, in this

11. Ibid., 1:43.
12. See ibid., 1:293–94.
13. Ibid., 1:42.
14. Schmithals, "Nachwort," 155.

sense, would be a set of statements about Jesus that one either affirms or denies. Preaching such a kerygma would be indistinguishable in principle from the teaching of general information about the world or the ostensibly neutral inquiry of the natural sciences.

As Bultmann understands it, the NT kerygma has an entirely different meaning and function. In his 1930 lecture on "The Christology of the New Testament," he begins by setting out his standard contrast between Greek and biblical thought, one that we already encountered in the above discussion of two different accounts of self-understanding. Bultmann argues that "historical research"—by which he means the liberal theological research of the late nineteenth and early twentieth centuries—"made the unconscious assumption" that the NT authors understood their teachings about Christ to be of the same character as Greek teachings about the nature of the cosmos. Liberal theologians thus "understood *the statements of the New Testament about Christ as statements about a world phenomenon*, about an entity whose 'nature' can be correctly described and whose relation to other world-entities is determinable positively and negatively."[15] Bultmann renders this same judgment with respect to traditional orthodox theologies that understand the NT statements in terms of the ecumenical creeds, but that was not his concern in Marburg during the early twentieth century. In his German academic context, it was liberal theology that presented the main challenge to a proper understanding of the kerygma.

The problem consisted in the way these theologians "naïvely measured the teaching of the New Testament by the modern scientific view of the world."[16] The result is that both Jesus and the statements made about him in the NT are

15. Bultmann, "Christology," 263.
16. Ibid.

objectified and treated with a certain scientific detachment. The liberals attempted to explain how faith in Jesus arose, and they did so with speculative theories about the impact of Jesus' personality, which supposedly inspired followers and awakened their imaginations through the power of his own faith in God and love for others. If this were the case, then the kerygma would simply be an account of how Jesus aroused faith and love in other people; it could "never *give me* that faith and love."[17] Faith based on a kerygma of this nature "would have been an illusion," because it would have been faith in other people's faith and not faith in Jesus himself.[18]

When we actually look at the NT, Bultmann points out, we see none of this. We instead find a singular focus on the necessity of faithful obedience to Jesus as the Christ who has made possible our salvation through his death and resurrection. This understanding of faith is directly tied to a particular understanding of the kerygma as the message that demands this obedience to Christ and elicits our response:

> To *have faith in Christ*, therefore, does not mean to hold particular opinions about his nature, although one can certainly have such opinions. Nor does it mean an imitative following of him, in the sense of allowing one's self to be drawn into his faith in God and his way of life. . . . What Paul calls faith first comes into existence after the death and resurrection of Christ—not before. Faith is certainly following Christ—but by accepting his cross, not at all in the sense of imitation, but as grasping the forgiveness and the possibility of life created by the cross. . . . Faith

17. Ibid., 267. Emphasis mine.
18. Ibid.

in Christ is complete submission under that which God has done in Christ. . . . What then is meant by *christology?* It is not the theoretical explanation of experiential piety; it is not speculation and teaching about the divine nature of Christ. It is proclamation; it is summons. It is the "teaching" that through Jesus our justification is achieved, that for our sakes he was crucified and is risen (Rom. 3.24f.; 4.25; 10.9; II Cor. 5.18f.).[19]

NT christology—which is the normative form of the kerygma—is not a set of theoretical propositions *about* Jesus, either in terms of his experiential influence (liberalism) or his metaphysical natures (orthodoxy). Instead, christology in the NT "is the proclamation of the event of Christ's coming," and "an understanding of the event requires not speculation but self-examination, radical consideration of the nature of one's own new existence."[20] The kerygma proclaims the Christ-event, and in the act of proclamation, it becomes the present actualization of the event, since "the preaching is a part of *the event itself*; Christ is present in the word."[21] And because, for Paul, the Christ-event is the justification-event—the coming of Christ being identical with the coming of faith (cf. Gal 2:16 and 3:24)[22]—it follows that *the kerygma makes Christ present by forgiving my sins*. This is why, as Ebeling says, "the meaning of the noun 'kerygma' oscillates between the content of proclamation and the act of proclamation."[23] In the kerygma, content and act are *identical.*

19. Ibid., 276–77.
20. Ibid., 279.
21. Ibid., 278.
22. See Congdon, "Trinitarian Shape," 245–46.
23. Ebeling, "Kerygma," 517.

The kerygma, therefore, is what Luther calls an "effective word" (*verbum efficax*)[24] or what Ebeling calls a "word-event."[25] By proclaiming Christ crucified for us, the kerygma is a proclamation, a word, in which Jesus Christ in his saving significance becomes an event that involves us here and now. In the kerygma, Christ himself confronts us as our Lord. And his lordship consists in the fact that he is the judge who simultaneously condemns our sin and forgives us. The kerygma thus encounters us as a disruptive word of judgment and grace:

> In the word, then, the salvation-occurrence is present. . . . For the proclaimed word is neither an enlightening *Weltanschauung* [worldview] flowing out in general truths, nor a merely historical account, which, like a reporter's story, "reminds" a public of decisive but by-gone facts. Rather, it is kerygma in the real sense—authorized, plenipotent proclamation, sovereign edict. . . . So it is, by nature, personal address which accosts each individual, throwing the person into question by rendering one's self-understanding problematic and demanding one's decision.[26]

The purpose of the kerygma is not to give us historical or metaphysical information—much less to give us a comprehensive worldview—but to interrupt our existence, to call us into question, to liberate us from sin for a new existence, a new self-understanding. This act of interruption and liberation is the essence of the kerygma. *Wherever this event of liberation occurs, there the kerygmatic word-event has taken place.*

24. See *LW*, 1:54.

25. Ebeling, *Theology and Proclamation*, 43; cf. Ebeling, "Word of God," 313–14.

26. *TNT*, 1:307, rev.

KERYGMA AND THEOLOGY

I use the language of "essence" deliberately. The kerygma is *essentially* a word-event, but this word-event can take a variety of historical forms. These forms are translations of the kerygma into the language and culture of a particular context. The most basic translation is the NT claim that Jesus is Lord or that Jesus is the Christ. But even this claim is *not* the kerygma itself, at least not directly. We instead must differentiate between kerygma, the word-event as such, and theology (in the broadest sense of the term) as the conceptualization of this event.[27]

Bultmann presents the question regarding the essence of the kerygma in distinction from theology most clearly in the passage from his letter to Heidegger in 1932 quoted above. The letter continues as follows:

> It is becoming increasingly apparent to me that the central problem of New Testament theology is to say what the Christian kerygma actually is. It is never present simply as something given, but is always formulated out of a particular believing understanding. Moreover, the New Testament, almost without exception, does not directly contain the kerygma, but rather certain statements (such as the Pauline doctrine of justification), in which the believing understanding of Christian being is developed, are based on the kerygma and refer back to it. What the kerygma is can never be said conclusively, but must constantly be found anew, because it is only actually the kerygma in the carrying out of the proclamation.[28]

27. The word "theology," for Bultmann, is an umbrella category that includes everything from the theological claims in Paul's epistles to church proclamation to the work of the systematic theologian.

28. Bultmann and Heidegger, *Briefwechsel*, 186.

According to Bultmann, the NT does not "directly contain" the kerygma, but rather the statements in the Bible are based on and bear witness to the kerygma. The distinction here between kerygma and scripture corresponds to Karl Barth's distinction between revelation and scripture. In his doctrine of revelation, Barth presents what he calls the "threefold form" of revelation as the word of God revealed (Jesus Christ), written (scripture), and proclaimed (contemporary preaching).[29] Barth's point is that God's self-revelation, definitively actualized in Christ, is qualitatively distinct from the written and spoken testimonies to it. The sovereign freedom of God precludes the collapse of revelation, as the act of God, into scripture, preaching, or theology as the human witnesses to revelation—scripture being the normative and authoritative witness over church preaching and teaching.

Like Barth, Bultmann refuses to collapse kerygma and theology, and he does so for similar reasons: God's otherness and nonobjectifiability, the lordship of Christ as the eschatological judge, our absolute dependence upon God's grace. However we articulate it, the distinction between God and the world means that the kerygma—if it is truly the *event* in which Christ speaks to us today and so communicates God's justifying grace to you and me—cannot be conflated with any single human articulation or interpretation. The distinction between kerygma and theology is a distinction between *direct* and *indirect* address: "We have made a distinction between christology that is kerygma as direct address and christology that is indirect address and is the theological explication of the new self-understanding of the believer, a critical-polemical explication made necessary by Paul's historical situation and carried out with the

---

29. *CD* 1.1:98–140.

use of a contemporary conceptuality."[30] In the kerygma, God addresses us directly; in theology, we speak and hear *about* God's direct address. This speaking and hearing about the kerygma takes place in a specific situation. The terms "historical situation" and "contemporary conceptuality" are Bultmann's way of saying that every presentation of the kerygma occurs in a particular cultural context—what Bultmann elsewhere calls a "world-picture" (*Weltbild*)[31]— and this context always involves a certain language or conceptuality. Every presentation of the kerygma, including those within scripture itself, is therefore already an interpretation:

> When, therefore, the science of New Testament theology seeks to present faith as the origin of the theological statements, it obviously must present the kerygma and the self-understanding opened up by it in which faith unfolds itself. And that is just where the problem lurks! For both the kerygma and faith's self-understanding always appear in the texts, so far as they are expressed in words and sentences, already interpreted in some particular way—i.e. in theological thoughts. Although there are single statements in the New Testament which can be designated as specifically kerygmatic, even they are always formulated in a particular theological conceptuality—take, for instance, that simplest sentence, "Jesus, Lord" (II Cor. 4:5), for it presupposes a particular understanding of the concept "Lord."[32]

30. Bultmann, "Christology," 280–81, rev.

31. Bultmann, "New Testament," 1.

32. *TNT*, 2:239, rev. This passage is from a 1950 essay on "The Problem of the Relation of Theology and Proclamation in the New Testament," included as an epilogue to his *Theology of the New Testament*.

This means that no presentation of the kerygma can be given universal significance or validity. Though Bultmann does not state so explicitly, scripture itself confirms this judgment by containing an abundance of kerygmatic translations that bear witness to the diversity of cultural contexts out of which the biblical texts and traditions arose. If this is true of scripture, it is even truer for the later creeds and confessions of the church, which are attempts to make sense of the church's proclamation within a different historical situation. None of these texts can presume to offer timeless and universal truths. They are *translations* of the truth into a specific cultural-linguistic form. But if we bind the kerygma to any single form, we bind God's act of revelation to a single cultural context, thereby implying that God does *not* speak to other contexts and communities. Insofar as Christianity presupposes that the gospel can be translated to every culture or language, it follows that the kerygma "can never be said conclusively" but has to be discovered ever anew.[33]

As counterintuitive as it may initially appear, the logical conclusion is that the kerygma is essentially *prelinguistic*. Bultmann indicates this by connecting the kerygma to one's new self-understanding: theology is the "explication of the new self-understanding of the believer," the latter being the human correlate of God's direct address in the kerygma.[34] In the previous chapter we saw that the new self-understanding of faith concerns an event that is not objectively available but has to be seized anew in the decision of obedience. Self-understanding takes place as a summons or address that places us outside of ourselves. The self-understanding of the believer is thus an act of the *will* rather than reason—and because it is entirely a gift, it is a

33. Bultmann and Heidegger, *Briefwechsel*, 186.
34. Bultmann, "Christology," 280, rev.

deed, not a work. The kerygma, understood as the divine act that elicits or opens up our new self-understanding, is thus an existential encounter that demands our fidelity; it is not a theoretical proposition that demands our assent. The responsibility of theology, broadly defined, is to make the transition from the encounter to the proposition, as well as to test the proposition in light of the encounter. These correspond, respectively, to the tasks of church proclamation and systematic theology. These tasks are indispensable to the kerygma, since every effort to *understand* it always requires appropriating the resources of one's context. While the kerygma itself is prelinguistic, it is constantly *becoming* linguistic, *becoming* conceptual, in every new moment.

We are now better able to understand why Bultmann says that "the central problem of New Testament theology is to say what the Christian kerygma actually is."[35] The kerygma is the heart of the Christian faith, and yet we cannot read the kerygma "off the page," so to speak. Instead, the task of New Testament theology follows the hints and whispers of the kerygma in the texts and traditions of Christianity. New Testament theology is by nature a *critical* science, according to Bultmann, since it is the practice of criticism that involves looking behind and beyond the words on the page.[36] As we will discuss further in a later chapter, Bultmann engages in a particular kind of criticism that he calls *Sachkritik*, which we can translate as "content criticism," or perhaps as "kerygmatic criticism," since the content that he is after is the kerygma itself.

---

35. Bultmann and Heidegger, *Briefwechsel*, 186.

36. As he says, "neither Paul's theology and christology nor that of any other Christian thinker can be understood uncritically," precisely because "every theological exposition of the saving event and of the Christian's existence is constructed with the use of contemporary conceptions" (Bultmann, "Christology," 279–80).

THE KERYGMATIC PARADOX

One may well ask at this point whether the kerygma has any actual content. If the kerygma is not directly identifiable even with the claim that Jesus is Lord, is there anything specifically Christian about the kerygma? This is the question raised by Bultmann's conservative critics. C. Kavin Rowe claims that "the kerygma for Bultmann is finally an abstraction" and "is at bottom only the fictitious creature of his intellect," while Wayne Meeks asserts that "the kerygma becomes little more than a formal operator, a ghostly signal."[37] On the other side are Bultmann's liberal critics, such as Fritz Buri and Schubert Ogden, who argue that Bultmann did not go far enough and should have moved from demythologizing to "dekerygmatizing."[38] The objection seems to be a forceful one. If we cannot tie the kerygma to a definite theological claim about Jesus being the Christ, then why remain a Christian theologian at all? Is Bultmann simply inconsistent?

We can only understand Bultmann's position by recognizing the delicate dialectic within which his theology unfolds. On the one hand, he is a Christian theologian who operates within the tradition of the church. For him it is axiomatic that the kerygma is a direct encounter with Jesus Christ who is present in the word of the gospel. He does not choose this ecclesial tradition from some ostensibly "neutral" position but accepts it as his contextual starting point. The church is the community that bears witness to the kerygma over time. He recognizes that one cannot affirm this kerygma without in some sense presupposing the church: "There is no faith in Christ that would not also be faith in the church as the bearer of the kerygma, that

37. Rowe, "Kerygma," 33; Meeks, "Problem," 221.
38. Buri, "Entmythologisierung," 85–101; Ogden, *Christ*, 110.

is, using the terminology of dogmatics, faith in the Holy Spirit."[39] For this reason, we must say: *historically speaking, there is no kerygma without the church*. At the same time, Bultmann resists any identification of the kerygma with the tradition of the church (e.g., the so-called "rule of faith") for the same reason that Barth refuses to collapse revelation into scripture or tradition. To conflate kerygma or revelation with some human reality would be to deify the creature. It would confuse the human witness with the divine object. The result would be yet another objectification of God. For this reason, we must also say: *normatively speaking, there is no church without the kerygma*. The church is the bearer of the kerygma, but the kerygma is what constitutes the church. The church only exists because there is a kerygma, an existential encounter with Christ, to which it bears witness. Bultmann's theology flows out of this paradox. His theology operates in the fluid dialectical space between these two claims. The first claim binds talk of the kerygma to Jesus Christ, while the second claim recognizes that the kerygma cannot be bound to any particular theological statement about Christ. This paradox runs throughout the entirety of Bultmann's work.

While the unity-in-distinction between the Jesus of history and the eschatological event of Christ is the paradigmatic form of this paradox, Bultmann's theology is arguably more concerned with another form of this paradox: the unity-in-distinction between the empirical church and the eschatological community. In the 1930s Bultmann was engaged in what is known as the "church struggle" (*Kirchenkampf*), which was a debate between the Confessing Church and the German Christians who were loyal to the Nazi Party. Bultmann was an early and active participant in the Confessing Church and his writings during this

39. Bultmann, "Primitive Christian Kerygma," 41, rev.

period attempt to undermine the German Christian position on various historical and hermeneutical grounds. He recognized that the German Christians had collapsed the kerygma into the cultural context of Germany; they had effectively dispensed with the second claim. For these Nazi supporters, the kerygma was essentially *German*. They had lost any sense of the church as an eschatological community. Against this Bultmann declares that the church "never becomes a piece of the world, but rather always maintains its transcendent, eschatological dimension. The preaching of the gospel always rings out *to* the people, never *from* the people."[40] Bultmann recognized that the only consistent way to oppose the German Christian position was to distinguish the kerygma from every cultural context and linguistic form, including those forms and contexts found in the biblical text itself, as well as in the history of theology.

The dialectical space between kerygma and culture, between eschatology and history, is the space of God's own freedom to speak ever anew. Without this paradox we end up binding God to a particular historical moment. We thereby close our ears to God's judgment on our past objectifications of revelation as well as to God's disclosure of new possibilities of faithful witness in new situations.

TOWARD A KERYGMATIC THEOLOGY OF RELIGIONS

If the kerygma is prelinguistic and not directly contained in or identified with any text or tradition, including the Christian scriptures, then is it possible that the kerygma can be found outside of Christianity altogether? Does Bultmann give us the resources for thinking about a theology of religions? Is salvation—however we define this—available

40. Bultmann, "Arier-Paragraph," 365.

outside of Christian faith? In asking these questions, we are moving beyond the scope of Bultmann's theology. As a self-consciously Christian theologian who abhorred all speculation, he rigorously remained within the strict limits of New Testament theology. His task, as he understood it, was to reflect on the content and meaning of the New Testament—no more and no less. At the same time, his work gestures in the direction of this line of inquiry.

The clearest evidence for a positive answer to the above questions appears in his 1952 response to criticisms of his demythologizing program, where he provides the following clarification of faith in God as existential self-understanding:

> Even faith in God as the Creator is not an already given certainty. . . . Such faith can be actualized genuinely only when I understand myself existentially here and now as God's creature, *which naturally need not come to consciousness as reflective knowledge.* Faith in God's omnipotence is not an already given conviction that there is a being who can do all things, but it can be actualized only existentially by subjecting myself to the power of God that subdues me here and now, *which, again, need not be raised to the level of explicit consciousness.*[41]

In the italicized clauses, Bultmann makes it clear that faith's self-understanding is actual and effective even if it does not become explicitly conscious, that is to say, even if it does not become an object of knowledge. A new kerygmatic self-understanding (i.e., faith) can occur *unconsciously*. This is not the first time he says something like this. Speaking in a 1941 lecture about believers receiving "a new understanding of themselves in unity with a new understanding of the word of

41. Bultmann, "On the Problem," 112. Emphasis mine.

God," he adds: "To be sure, this new self-understanding can be present in an unreflective form. . . . Theology is nothing other than the reflective, methodical unfolding of the understanding of the word of God and of the self-understanding disclosed through this word and given in faith."[42] In a way, Bultmann is making a rather pedestrian distinction between faith itself and thinking about faith. What makes his position somewhat novel with respect to traditional Christian orthodoxy is the claim that the former can occur apart from one's conscious, reflective awareness.

There is a connection here to Bultmann's hermeneutics, a topic I will take up in more detail in a later chapter. According to Bultmann, every interpretation of a text presupposes "the life relation of the interpreter to the subject matter that is—directly or indirectly—expressed in the text."[43] A person can only understand a text about music, for example, if she already has some prior understanding of what music is. She already has a life-relation to music, which means that music is already, in some sense, a meaningful part of her life. A prior life-relation or preunderstanding is the presupposition for all interpretation. But this life-relation, Bultmann says, need not be conscious: "Naturally, my life relation to the subject matter can be utterly naive and unreflective, and in the process of understanding, in the interpretation, it can be raised to the level of consciousness and clarified."[44] The similarity between this statement and the ones quoted above regarding the unreflective or unconscious self-understanding of faith is obvious. Does that mean an unconscious faith is the hermeneutical presupposition for understanding revelation?

42. Bultmann, "Theology as Science," 57.
43. Bultmann, "Problem of Hermeneutics," 74.
44. Ibid., 75.

This leads us to one of the most complicated areas of Bultmann's theology: the topic of natural theology. According to Bultmann, the understanding of revelation requires a preunderstanding of revelation. Understanding the word of God in scripture and preaching "presupposes a coherent life-complex in which the one who understands and what is understood belong together."[45] But what does this mean? First, it means that revelation encounters a person who already has a history, who belongs already to a particular situation in history. Revelation neither encounters nor creates a blank slate. There is a continuity between the person before and after faith. Second, and more importantly, the existence of the person prior to faith is "questionable." Her natural self-understanding is the self-understanding of a *sinner*, though she does not know this yet; the "questionableness" of this natural self-understanding "only becomes clear as such in the understanding of existence in faith."[46] Revelation answers this questionableness by overcoming it, replacing one's natural self-understanding with a new self-understanding. In his later writings, Bultmann pushes this further and speaks of an "existential knowledge of God" in the "question about God" that belongs to human existence as such:

> If it is objected that we human beings cannot know who God is and hence also cannot know what God's act means prior to God's revelation, the proper reply is that we can very well know who God is in the question about God. Unless our existence were moved (consciously or unconsciously) by the question about God in the sense of Augustine's "Thou hast made us for thyself, and our heart is restless until it rests in

45. Bultmann, "Problem of 'Natural Theology,'" 315.
46. Ibid., 317.

thee," we would not be able to recognize God as God in any revelation. There is an existential knowledge of God present and alive in human existence in the question about "happiness" or "salvation" or about the meaning of the world and of history, insofar as this is the question about the authenticity of our own existence. If the right to describe this question as the question about God is first acquired by faith in God's revelation, still the phenomenon as such is a relation to the subject matter of revelation.[47]

Bultmann's talk of being moved *unconsciously* by the question about God certainly brings us closer to the unconscious faith described in the passages above, but even here he is only referring to the *question* and not to the answer. The question about God is not itself a new self-understanding, even if it involves "knowledge . . . of a transcendent reality."[48] In the passages from 1941 and 1952 quoted above, Bultmann is speaking about the unconsciousness of the *answer* that is faith's new self-understanding.

So where does that leave us? It is certainly possible that Bultmann's rather opaque claims regarding the possibility of an unconscious faith in God are supposed to be a reference to the preunderstanding of revelation found in Augustine's "restless heart." Or perhaps they are supposed to be a kind of Tillichian "faith in the presence of the unconditioned in the conditioned," even though, besides being conscious and reflective, Bultmann expressly denies this is the same as "Christian faith in God."[49] But taken at face value, they seem to suggest that true Christian self-understanding can occur unconsciously. And since, as we have already seen,

47. Bultmann, "Problem of Hermeneutics," 87.
48. Bultmann, "Protestant Theology," 333.
49. Ibid., 333–34.

the kerygma is essentially prelinguistic, the possibility of an unreflective or unconscious faith is to be expected. It would entail, as Bultmann suggests, an existential understanding of oneself as a creature who is absolutely dependent upon the power of God. Though Bultmann refuses to speculate, presumably one might gain this self-understanding through a boundary experience, such as a moment of crisis or an encounter with beauty or death. His reference to unconscious faith in 1952 occurs in the context of speaking about God's action in the world as paradoxically identical with natural and historical occurrences. Faith in God is "genuine faith in wonders," which are not objectively visible but are seen with the eyes of faith.[50] An unreflective faith may be a new self-understanding—a personal liberation from the static regularity of life—that comes through witnessing an event that one can only understand as a divine wonder. In responding to this liberating moment, one has responded to the kerygma.[51]

Is it possible to see here the basis for a Bultmannian theology of religions? We have to be cautious, since Bultmann himself rejects the idea "that the Christian faith consists in the purer disclosure of the knowledge of God which exists in all religion." He denies any understanding of the kerygma that would make it a link, even if the highest, in "a development of religion or a development of the history of thought."[52] As a Christian theologian, he insists on the absolute uniqueness of the Christian kerygma; it is strictly a divine act, never an element in the evolution of

50. Bultmann, "On the Problem," 113.

51. There are similarities worth exploring between Bultmann and Karl Rahner's concept of "anonymous Christian" and Dietrich Bonhoeffer's concept of "unconscious Christianity." For more on those latter views, see Kelly, "Unconscious Christianity."

52. Bultmann, "Problem of 'Natural Theology,'" 322.

human religious consciousness. At the same time, because this kerygma occurs outside of reflective Christian faith, it is possible to find genuine faith in other religions, as well as in those who deny religious belief altogether. But because such faith is unconscious, it is only visible to those who have a conscious faith in Jesus as the Christ, who thus have the criterion for what is authentically kerygmatic, "for God is accessible only to faith responsive to revelation."[53] From this perspective, theology has the task not only of clarifying the nature and object of conscious faith, but also of seeing and affirming the moments of *unconscious* faith, wherever and whenever they occur.[54]

QUESTIONS FOR REFLECTION

1. Where have you encountered the kerygma outside of the (visible) church? Where have you encountered unconscious faith?

2. If the kerygma is not directly identifiable with scripture, how should we understand the authority and significance of the biblical text? What implications does this have for biblical exegesis?

53. Ibid.

54. Bultmann, we should note, was a firm opponent of every universalism, Christian or otherwise, because of the way universalisms speak in the abstract about humanity as such. For this reason, universalism is impossible on the soil of dialectical theology, at least as Bultmann understands it, which can only speak of God in connection to the concrete historicity of the person whom God affects and encounters. Bultmann criticized Barth on this very issue in their debate over the interpretation of Romans 5, one of the classic texts of Christian universalism (Bultmann, "Adam," 158). Bultmann assumes that every universalism undermines the existential decision that he sees as indispensable to any Christian account of salvation. Whether one can conceive of a universalism that upholds this decision of faith is not a possibility that Bultmann considers.

3. How would Bultmann's understanding of the relation between kerygma and theology affect the discipline of systematic theology? What implications would it have for the creation, reception, and interpretation of church confessions?

4. How might it reorient the mission of the church if we think of word and sacrament as aiding us in the work of discerning unreflective faith in the world around us?

6

HISTORY

THE HISTORIAN AND THE BELIEVER

IT IS VIRTUALLY IMPOSSIBLE to understand German theology in the nineteenth and twentieth centuries without some familiarity with the concept of history. Today we take the study of history for granted, even if the actual presuppositions, methods, and results of this research are foreign to most people. The idea of history and the possibility of researching it are as natural to us as typing on a computer. Looking back so many decades later, it is almost impossible for people today to understand how novel and revolutionary the very idea of history was.

The modern era, one could argue with justification, is the era in which historical consciousness arose. By historical consciousness we mean the consciousness of the past (and, by extension, the present) as an object of scientific inquiry, alongside other objects, such as the natural world. "This revolution in consciousness found its formal expression in the creation of a new science, history." The job of the historian was to present the objective, scientific "facts" about "what really happened." "Description, impartiality, and objectivity were the ideals, and the rhetorical phrase and the value judgment were looked upon with disdain."[1] This new enterprise, marked by an uncompromising method, was inherently critical in nature, exposing as false and fictional what many people had held for centuries to be true and factual. Theologians in the late nineteenth and early twentieth centuries saw that this new discipline had radical implications for Christian faith:

> If the theologian regards the Scriptures as supernaturally inspired, the historian must assume that the Bible is intelligible only in terms of its historical context and is subject to the same principles of interpretation and criticism that are applied to other ancient literature. If the theologian believes that the events of the Bible are the results of the supernatural intervention of God, the historian regards such an explanation as a hindrance to true historical understanding. If the theologian believes that the events upon which Christendom rests are unique, the historian assumes that those events, like all events, are analogous to those in the present and that it is only on this assumption that statements about them can be assessed at all. If the theologian believes on faith that certain events occurred, the historian regards all historical claims as having only a greater or lesser degree of probability, and he regards the attachment of faith to these claims as a corruption of historical judgment.[2]

Between the historian and the believer there seems to be an unbridgeable divide.

---

1. Harvey, *Historian*, 4.
2. Ibid., 4–5.

Christian theologians have responded to the divide between faith and history in four main ways:

1. *Denying the problem of history*. Some refuse to accept historical consciousness. This would include those who insist that scripture and the orthodox tradition are universally true and authoritative precisely as given, and that any attempt to test these traditions and texts against other criteria is a faithless enterprise. The only true history is the one narrated in the Bible or declared by the church's teaching office.

2. *Adjusting faith to fit history*. Other theologians have embraced history wholeheartedly, going so far as to reconstruct the entirety of Christian faith on the grounds given to us in historical science. Ernst Troeltsch is the paradigmatic representative of this view. He insisted that Christianity had to enter the purging fires of historical science without reserve in order to emerge with a religion that would be meaningful for the modern world.

3. *Using history to support faith*. More recently, theologians have turned to history to *defend* traditional Christianity. This started to occur in the second half of the twentieth century with the rise of the so-called "third quest" of the historical Jesus. This school of thought rejects the naturalistic assumptions of the historical method as taught by the likes of Troeltsch. Proponents of this view, such as N. T. Wright, claim that one can use modern historical methodology to support the veracity of the biblical narrative, though not necessarily the validity of certain later traditions.

4. *Differentiating between faith and history*. The final view accepts historical consciousness but denies the competition with faith by differentiating between faith and history. According to this view, theological knowledge and historical knowledge are qualitatively different and cannot be placed in tension with each other. One can carry out this

position by (a) denying that faith has any historical component at all or (b) affirming that faith is related to history but in a way that is inaccessible to historical science.

For our purposes here, we are interested in position 4b.[3] While it is a view that has roots much earlier, it rose to prominence as a solution to the faith-history problem thanks to the 1892 publication of Martin Kähler's classic work, *Der sogenannte historische Jesus und der geschichtliche, biblische Christus* (ET *The So-Called Historical Jesus and the Historic Biblical Christ*). Kähler made the all-important distinction between *Historie* and *Geschichte*, and in doing so he became "the prophetic forerunner of what developed more fully only in the twentieth century."[4] Carl Braaten thus observes that Kähler "can be viewed as a forerunner of either Karl Barth or Rudolf Bultmann," since both propound versions of 4b.[5]

HISTORIE AND GESCHICHTE

In order to understand German theology in the twentieth century, one must understand the distinction between *Historie* and *Geschichte*. Colloquially, the two words are synonymous, and both can be translated accurately into English as "history." The word *Historie*, like the English cognate, comes from the Greek word ἱστορία (*historia*), which means a narration. *Geschichte* is a Germanic equivalent that originated in the Old High German of the eleventh century; it also means narration or story and is related to *Geschehen*, which means an occurrence or event. With the

3. Given that Christianity stands or falls based on the relation to Jesus of Nazareth, position 4a could not be considered Christian in any meaningful sense.

4. Tillich, *Perspectives*, 215.

5. Kähler, *So-Called Historical Jesus*, 2.

rise of history as a scientific discipline and the creation of the historical method, it became necessary to differentiate between the history told in traditional narratives and myths and the history reconstructed by the historians. *Geschichte* was assigned to the former and *Historie* to the latter. A *historisch* fact is therefore a bare occurrence that lends itself to neutral historical analysis, while a *geschichtlich* event might be the same occurrence as it is given meaning by human beings, through philosophical or theological interpretation or through integration into the course of human affairs. Both words are translated as "historical," but they carry distinctly different meanings.[6]

We can illustrate this by looking at some passages in Bultmann's writings. Take, for example, the statement from Bultmann's 1955 Gifford Lectures on *History and Eschatology*—published in English in 1957 and in German in 1958— where Bultmann is speaking about secularization. He says that secularization was able to take place "after an epoch of critical history [*Historie*], which was purely interested in establishing historical [*historischen*] facts, had done its work and awakened the question of the meaning of history [*Geschichte*], according to the interpretation of historical [*historischen*] facts."[7] Bultmann connects *Historie* with

6. An earlier generation of German translation translated *historisch* as "historical" and *geschichtlich* as "historic," but that convention did not last, in large part because the words are not always used in this strictly differentiated way. *Geschichte* is sometimes used to refer to *Historie* even by those theologians, including Bultmann, who distinguish between the two meanings of history. Today, both sets of words are generally translated as "history" or "historical," and if the German is not provided in brackets to clarify the meaning, the reader has to discern the intended meaning from the context.

7. Bultmann, *Geschichte*, 71–72. Cf. Bultmann, *History*, 62. The English version reads: "after an epoch of critical historical research interested only in establishing historical facts, when the question about meaning in history awakes anew and with it an interest in

facts that can be established by critical historical methods and associates *Geschichte* with the interpretation of these facts and the awakening of meaning. This distinction carries through all of his writings. In his *Theology of the New Testament*, Bultmann argues that the eschatological community constituted by the inbreaking event of Christ is "not simply the historical [*historische*] successor and heir of the empirical-historical [*empirisch-historischen*] Israel but the heir of the ideal Israel, so to say, the people of God which the historical Israel was indeed called to be. . . . But this contrast with the historical Israel, this eschatological break in history [*Geschichte*], does not mean discontinuity in the history of salvation [*Heilsgeschichte*] but precisely the opposite—continuity."[8] Bultmann frequently juxtaposes *historisch* and *empirisch*, since the two words are synonymous for him: the historical method is only able to access what is empirical and observable. This is why the Christ-event is a break only in *Geschichte*, a break in history as it has meaning for human beings in the world. And that is also why the eschatological community of faith in Christ can be discontinuous with the Israel of *Historie* but continuous with the Israel of *Geschichte*—specifically, the Israel of the *Heilsgeschichte*, which is history understood theologically as the history of God's dealings with humankind.[9] In support of this reading, Bultmann draws on Paul's statement in

---

interpreting the facts." Notice that *Historie* is rendered here as "historical research," which correctly conveys the meaning of the term in order to avoid ambiguity.

8. *TNT*, 1:97, rev.

9. Though Bultmann uses the word *Heilsgeschichte* here, it is important to understand that he does *not* belong to the *Heilsgeschichte* school of New Testament interpretation (e.g., Oscar Cullmann), which understands Christ as the climactic midpoint of redemptive history.

1 Corinthians 10:18, where he speaks of "Israel according to the flesh" ('Ισραὴλ κατὰ σάρκα).

The connection between "according to the flesh" and *Historie* is a key feature of Bultmann's theology, and it plays the most significant role in his discussion of the so-called quest for the historical (i.e., *historisch*) Jesus. Bultmann arrived on the theological scene in the years following the 1906 publication of Albert Schweitzer's devastating critique of the nineteenth-century research on the "life of Jesus." Schweitzer showed that the quest to find the truly "historical" Jesus behind the traditions of the church had been a complete failure. Bultmann explains why in his early lecture on "Liberal Theology and the Latest Theological Movement":

> But to what result has the course of historical criticism actually led? If it was at first directed by a confidence that such critical research would free men from the burden of dogmatics and lead to a comprehension of the real figure of Jesus on which faith could be based, this confidence soon proved to be delusion. Historical research can never lead to any result which could serve as a basis for faith, for *all its results have only relative validity*. How widely the pictures of Jesus presented by liberal theologians differ from one another! How uncertain is all knowledge of "the historical Jesus"! Is he really within the scope of our knowledge? Here research ends with a large question mark—and here it *ought* to end.[10]

Bultmann found in the dialectical theology of Barth an explanation for *why* it failed. Bultmann quotes Barth's response to Adolf von Harnack in 1923, where Barth says that "critical-historical study means the deserved and necessary

10. Bultmann, "Liberal Theology," 30.

end of *the* 'foundations' of [faith's] knowledge, which are no foundations at all because they are not laid by God. Those who still do not know . . . that we *cannot* any longer know Christ according to the flesh should let themselves be taught by the critical science of the Bible."[11] Barth draws the connection in this letter between the "historical Jesus" and Christ "according to the flesh," a connection he first makes in his *Epistle to the Romans* when discussing Romans 1:3.[12] Commenting on Barth's response to von Harnack, Bultmann says that historical criticism "frees us from bondage to every historical construction which is within the scope of historical science, and brings us to the realization that the world which faith wills to grasp is absolutely unattainable by means of scientific research."[13] Critical historical research is necessary, therefore, because it frees us from the temptation to construct a Christ according to the flesh, which is not the Christ that faith knows, as Paul indicates in his letter to the Corinthians. And as we saw in a previous chapter, Bultmann connects thinking "according to the flesh" with epistemological objectification. The attempt to reconstruct the object of faith by means of historical research objectifies God as something objectively present.

The differentiation between the *historisch* Jesus and the *geschichtlich* Christ—between the Jesus reconstructed by history and the Christ known by faith—is thus a kind of red thread tying together the whole body of Bultmann's work. Several years later, for instance, he criticizes Emanuel Hirsch for presenting Jesus Christ as a historical fact "which is *given* objectively. . . . The result is 'Christ after the flesh.'"[14] Later in the same essay he adds the famous remark:

11. Barth, *Offene Briefe*, 66–67.
12. Barth, *Epistle*, 29.
13. Bultmann, "Liberal Theology," 31.
14. Bultmann, "On the Question," 124.

I have never yet felt uncomfortable with my critical radicalism; on the contrary, I have been entirely comfortable. But I often have the impression that my conservative New Testament colleagues feel very uncomfortable, for I see them perpetually engaged in salvage operations. I calmly let the fire burn, for I see that what is consumed is only the fanciful portraits of Life-of-Jesus theology, and that means nothing other than "Christ after the flesh" (Χριστὸς κατὰ σάρκα).[15]

ESCHATOLOGY AND HISTORY

Bultmann's reflection on *Historie* and *Geschichte* is not merely negative in nature. While he emphatically denies that historical research gains us access to the object of faith, this does not mean he removes faith from history altogether, nor does it mean such research has nothing positive to contribute to faith. Critics of Bultmann have not been as sensitive to this point. Even though his radicalism consumes the life-of-Jesus research, Bultmann is not a historical skeptic. He is confident we can say quite a few things about the Jesus of history, not only that he existed and was crucified, but that he was a wonder-working exorcist and apocalyptic prophet who expected the imminent arrival of the messiah. Many of the statements in the Gospel accounts he traces back to what he calls the "old tradition."[16] This much is evident from reading *The History of the Synoptic Tradition* and especially his *Theology of the New Testament*. What interests me here, however, is not the relation of *history* to faith—a relation that Bultmann views as largely though not entirely negative—but rather the relation of *faith* to history.

15. Ibid., 132.
16. *TNT*, 1:3.

For Bultmann, everything depends on properly order-
ing faith and history. The liberal theologians placed history
before faith, and the result was a Christ who was the mir-
ror image of the historian.[17] But the problem is not limited
to the liberal theologians of the nineteenth century. It is
a dilemma faced by any approach that tries to define the
object of faith on the basis of what is objectively present:
the natural world, social or political life, ancient tradition,
etc. This includes more traditional salvation-historical approaches that see Christ as the climax of a long history of
redemption, since here, too, Christ's identity is defined in
advance by the history of salvific expectation. The continuity of the Christian community with Israel is only given
within *Geschichte*, that is, in faith; it cannot be seen on the
level of *Historie*. "The continuity is not a continuity growing out of history," Bultmann says, "but is one created by
God."[18] The problem of faith and history is therefore the
problem of natural theology. And for Bultmann, natural
theology of every kind is ruled out not because it proves
unsuccessful in the end, but because it contradicts the very
nature of God. If we are going to understand the relation
between faith and history, we can only do so *from within the
perspective of faith*.

How then does faith relate to history? In order to answer this question we must return to the topic with which
we began: eschatology. Second Temple Judaism understood
history in light of eschatology, but theirs was an apocalyptic
eschatology based on the imminent expectation of God's
reign. The Christian community appropriated this eschatology but applied it to the person of Jesus. Faith thus originates in response to the revelation of God that has already

17. Today, in light of the third quest, we might say it is now the
conservatives who are liable to this critique.

18. Bultmann, *History*, 35.

occurred in Christ. For the community of faith, Christ is the eschatological event through whom "history [*Geschichte*] is divided into two parts. He is the turning point of the aeons, the *krisis*. The new aeon has broken in. That is, by faith in him the possibility is given of getting free, not of something past but of the past as such."[19] Being free of the "past as such" does not mean being free of *history*—since the inbreaking of the new aeon occurs in a historical occurrence—but rather free of empirical history (*Historie*) as a constraint on God's saving action:

> Christian faith is *faith in the revelation of God* . . . . That is, it is faith in *an historical* [*geschichtliches*] *fact*. But it is such that this fact as objectively verifiable is not revelation. Otherwise faith would be historical [*historisches*] knowledge or the uncritical acceptance of historical [*historischen*] information, in short, a *fides historica* . . . . The less faith is such a *fides historica*, the more it is the certainty that through the historical [*historische*] fact of Jesus Christ history [*Geschichte*] is marked as a history of salvation [*Geschichte des Heils*]. It is marked by the fact that through Jesus Christ, the one proclaimed, forgiveness of sins is preached, and I as justified enter upon my present moment.[20]

Though the subtle use of the terms *historisch* and *geschichtlich* in this passage is difficult to convey in English, Bultmann's point is clear: Christian faith is faith in a historical fact, but this fact is historical for faith in the sense of *Geschichte* rather than *Historie*. To have faith in Christ is fundamentally different from believing, for example, that Caesar crossed the Rubicon on January 10 in 49 BCE. It is

19. Bultmann, *What Is Theology?*, 134.
20. Ibid., 129–30.

even different from believing that Jesus was born in Bethlehem or that he was crucified by Roman soldiers. That is merely *historisch* knowledge, which is not, and cannot be, the object of justifying faith. If the Christ-event were *historisch*, then it would have been the public arrival of God's reign expected by Jewish apocalyptic. Since Christians believe that this event occurred for faith, and is not generally visible to all people, it follows that the coming of Christ was *geschichtlich*.

Christian faith, according to Bultmann, believes that in Jesus "the new aeon has broken in," but this new aeon is not empirical for the same reason that God is not empirical. The new aeon is a singularly divine act; it is what Bultmann also calls revelation and justification. This eschatological event—which the Christian tradition identifies especially with the Easter event—places all of empirical history in a new light, including Jesus' own history. Apart from Easter, Jesus is only another apocalyptic prophet, and his death is that of yet another Roman criminal. The death of Jesus becomes the event of salvation only retrospectively on the basis of Easter faith. The cross can "be understood as a historical event that is the salvation event insofar as it is seen, not in an objectifiable world-historical context but in its significance."[21] The significance of the cross, according to Bultmann, is what the tradition names the resurrection, since "faith in the resurrection is nothing other than faith in the cross as the salvation event, as the cross of Christ."[22] The resurrection "says much more than that a dead person has returned to life in this world. It is an object of faith because it is an eschatological event."[23] When the kerygma proclaims that Jesus is the Christ, that the crucified one is

21. Bultmann, "New Testament," 33.

22. Ibid., 39.

23. Ibid., 38.

risen, it proclaims that Jesus, in his historicity, is present and effective today in the preached word. Easter faith is eschatological in the sense that it believes that Jesus is not lost to the past but remains ever present and future; he is always ahead of us, and so always with us.

The kerygma thus "speaks simultaneously of the eschatological occurrence and of an historical occurrence. The question is whether this paradoxical character was maintained."[24] The paradox is maintained only if the eschatological and the historical are paradoxically *identical*, that is, if the eschatological is something that occurs not *alongside* the historical but rather *in* the historical and thus *as* the historical, albeit in a way accessible only to faith. Bultmann grounds this notion of paradoxical identity in the NT itself, particularly in the Johannine notion of the Logos made flesh. According to the witness of John, the deity of Jesus is not something we find beside but only *in* his humanity: "It is in his sheer humanity that he is the Revealer. . . . This is the paradox that runs through the whole Gospel: the δόξα [glory] is not to be seen *alongside* the σάρξ [flesh], nor *through* it as through a window; it is to be seen in the σάρξ and nowhere else."[25] For Bultmann, the paradoxical relation between divine glory and human flesh in Christ is the norm for understanding the relation between eschatology and history in general. On this basis Bultmann criticizes the mythical presentation of the Christ-event in the Gospel narratives and the later Christian tradition for placing the cross and resurrection in a sequential order, so that the eschatological event of resurrection occurs alongside the *historisch* event of the cross as a second ostensibly *historisch* occurrence.[26] Separating the two events in this

24. *TNT*, 2:126.

25. Bultmann, *Das Evangelium*, 40–41.

26. Bultmann, "New Testament," 32.

way, like separating the humanity and deity of Christ, denies the paradox and threatens the integrity of Christian faith. On the one hand, it would mean the resurrection is an objectively verifiable fact, in which case it could not be the divine act of revelation, since the God who forgives sins is nonobjectifiable. On the other hand, it would mean the cross is not an eschatological event, in which case Jesus' death would be merely one death among others, without saving significance for people today. Only by maintaining the paradox are we able to do justice to both cross and resurrection, humanity and divinity, history and eschatology.

To summarize, Bultmann differentiates between history and eschatology so that they paradoxically coincide as a single event. Faith remains related at all times to the historical, but because they relate paradoxically, the access to the historical is determined by the eschatological. On this basis Bultmann criticizes the various quests for the "historical Jesus" for either dispensing with the eschatological altogether or trying to begin with the historical in order to reach the eschatological, the product of which is a deity constructed "according to the flesh." His theology is equally a challenge to those theologies that confuse the historical and the eschatological. The result of such confusion is mythology, and it appears not only in scripture but also in contemporary church teaching and proclamation. That leads us to the subject of our next chapter.

QUESTIONS FOR REFLECTION

1. Can historical research confirm Christian truth claims? If historical research regarding the Bible were to verify some, or even most, of the main events in the NT, would this provide grounds for faith?

2. Can historical research disprove Christian truth claims? What would count as conclusive evidence against faith? What if the bones of Jesus were found and verified? What if it were verified that Jesus never lived?

3. If the eschatological event is not only past but also present, how does the eschatological event of Christ relate to our particular histories today? How is the paradox maintained in this contemporary relation between eschatology and history?

7

MYTH

WHILE BULTMANN IS ASSOCIATED positively with the concept of kerygma, he is associated negatively with the concept
of myth. Despite his astonishingly wide range of theological
and exegetical writings, he is known to most people solely
by a lecture he gave in 1941 on "New Testament and Mythology," which announced his program of demythologizing.[1]
Since that time virtually all engagement with his work has
been filtered through one's prior judgment regarding the
validity or invalidity of this program, and at the heart of
that judgment is a prior assumption regarding the question
of myth—specifically, what it is, whether it has a place in
biblical interpretation, and whether that place is positive,
negative, or both. Many people assume that Bultmann
views myth wholly in a negative light, and so criticisms of
Bultmann have often taken the form of a defense of myth.

1. In English discussions, Bultmann's program is often called
"demythologization." This is a technically valid translation of the
German *Entmythologisierung*, but the gerund is more accurate.
Moreover, "demythologization" subtly misconstrues what is an active
and open hermeneutic as something fixed and static; it suggests that
there is an end to the process, when in fact Bultmann understands
his program to be something that is constantly taking place in each
situation.

In this chapter I will briefly explain what he means by myth, showing that he views it both positively and negatively. Understanding this concept will go a long way towards clarifying his hermeneutical program, to which we will turn in the following chapter.

MYTH AS THE VEHICLE OF REVELATION

Before we can understand the problem, we first need to understand what Bultmann affirms about myth. He refers to this in various writings as the "real intention" of myth. What is this intention and how do we gain access to it?

Bultmann begins by defining myth in contrast to science. The contrast between them, he argues, is absolute and qualitative, rather than relative and quantitative. Myth is "not simply a primitive form of science" that becomes obsolete with the arrival of modern science; it is instead a fundamentally different way of thinking about oneself— particularly in relation to the world.[2] Whereas science examines the world from a certain objective distance, myth "does not know this distance from the cosmos that belongs to the scientific vision, but rather it considers itself in direct encounter with the cosmos."[3] Myth overcomes the distance between the knowing subject and the known object. The one who tells the myth is herself involved in the story. Put another way, myth is existentially oriented. In regarding certain phenomena as numinous in character—for example, attributing certain occurrences to divine or demonic agents—myth makes them explicable and tolerable. Unlike science, which seeks to understand the totality of the cosmos, myth is "concerned with the grasping of what is individual and particular, what is meaningful for existence

2. Bultmann, "On the Concept of 'Myth,'" 854.
3. Ibid.

here and now." This is seen in the "naïve carelessness" with which myths find themselves in contradictions regarding specific mythical statements.

Bultmann thus argues that myth was a particularly appropriate vehicle for communicating the truth of revelation in the biblical texts. He makes this point most clearly in the conclusion to a 1927 essay on the latest research on the Gospel of John. Here he again contrasts myth and science:

> Myth is not primarily a primitive scientific world-explanation that could be criticized by a more highly developed science. . . . In truth myth expresses how human beings understand themselves in their being in the world; it expresses this by conceptualizing out of the longing of human beings a picture of their dreams and desires. . . . Myth expresses the insight that human beings are strangers who are lost in the world and cannot find their bearings, who cannot secure themselves as authentic beings through rational reflection.[4]

The attempt to criticize myth on the basis of modern science misses the true nature and meaning of myth, which brings to expression the truth of the human predicament. Myth speaks of something far more profound and significant than science's attempt to understand the nature of the world. Since the Gospels are concerned with the sin and salvation of human beings as revealed in Christ, it is appropriate for them to make use of myth to fulfill their function as church proclamation. At the same time, Bultmann is emphatic that myth does not determine revelation, but rather revelation determines the appropriation of myth: "The Gospel of John itself is not mythology; it only uses the forms of expression of myth with a sovereign certainty,

4. Bultmann, *Theologie als Kritik*, 214.

along with the forms of the older Gospel tradition, in order to present its understanding of the revelation of God in Jesus."[5] Myth is not essential to the kerygma, but myth is a fitting vehicle for the kerygma. Unlike science, "myth knows the idea of revelation."[6]

These statements may come as a surprise to those who are accustomed to hearing that Bultmann is the avowed enemy of myth. Nothing could be further from the truth. Bultmann, in fact, defends the truthfulness of myth over against a modern scientistic world inclined to relegate myth to the dustbin of antiquity. At the same time, he does not collapse the kerygma into myth, and it is this differentiation between revelation and the mythical forms of expression in scripture that funds his program of demythologizing. In what follows I will briefly describe two dimensions to this differentiation: the cultural and the epistemological.

THE MYTHICAL WORLD-PICTURE

Most people encounter Bultmann for the first time in the famous opening line of his programmatic essay on demythologizing: "The world picture of the New Testament is a mythical world picture."[7] He goes on to give a list of examples, including the well-known "three-decker world" with heaven above and hell below, the intervention of supernatural powers, and the expectation of an imminent cosmic catastrophe. All of this, he says, belongs to an irretrievable past that we cannot and need not repristinate:

> Insofar as it is mythological talk it is incredible to men and women today because for them the mythical world picture is a thing of the past.

5. Ibid., 214.

6. Ibid., 215.

7. Bultmann, "New Testament," 1.

> Therefore, contemporary Christian proclama-
> tion is faced with the question whether, when it
> demands faith from men and women, it expects
> them to acknowledge this mythical world pic-
> ture of the past. If this is impossible, it then has
> to face the question whether the New Testament
> proclamation has a truth that is independent
> of the mythical world picture, in which case it
> would be the task of theology to demythologize
> the Christian proclamation.[8]

The key phrase here is that "the mythical world picture is a thing of the past." Bultmann does not say that myth is false or that it is antithetical to faith; he says, in effect, that it is culturally *foreign*. Myth belongs to an alien time and place. Myth was, as we saw above, the form of expression that the biblical writers used to understand revelation in their particular context. The question that Bultmann poses is whether and how we can understand revelation *today* using new forms of expression.

Many readers of Bultmann are put off by his delib-erately provocative language in the programmatic essay. Much of the popular commentary stalls upon reaching his famous line: "We cannot use electric lights and radios and, in the event of illness, avail ourselves of modern medical and clinical means and at the same time believe in the spirit and wonder world of the New Testament."[9] Surely Bult-mann is mistaken, we might say, since many people clearly *do* use modern medicine and yet still believe in the wonder world of the Bible. This response misses the point. Bult-mann does not think that belief in the wonder world of the NT can be isolated from the cultural context in which that belief comes to expression, just as the use of the radio and

8. Ibid., 2–3.
9. Ibid., 4.

modern medicine likewise presupposes a distinct cultural context, as missionaries to remote tribes today understand well. Indeed, he would say this spirit and wonder world is not even an element of the NT kerygma, since it was a world-picture shared by everyone in that cultural context. It was as natural to them as our belief today in the capacity of scientists to discover the biological cause of a person's illness. The early Christian apostles necessarily made use of their world-picture in bearing witness to what God had done in Jesus of Nazareth, but that can be no more essential to the kerygma than the use of Greek or Aramaic.

Bultmann raises the same issue from other less inflammatory angles. The most important of these is eschatology. As we discussed already in the first chapter, the notion that the end of the age was near at hand, indeed that it would arrive within their own lifetimes, was central to ancient Jewish and Christian proclamation. Such preaching was mythological because it "was developed in conceptions which are no longer intelligible today."[10] Bultmann could have just as easily said: *one cannot prepare for retirement and take out insurance policies and at the same time believe in the apocalyptic world of the New Testament.* The point is the same: the cultural world-picture of the NT is simply incompatible with the common sense belief of people today that world history will carry on indefinitely—most likely until some environmental or cosmological disaster ends human life on this planet. Modern Christians, given their world-picture, necessarily differentiate between history and eschatology, whereas the earliest Christian community did not make any clear distinction. History and eschatology blurred together in a farrago of the immanent and the transcendent. This manifests itself in the early church's inchoate christology, where "the historical and the mythical [i.e., the eschato-

10. Bultmann, *Jesus Christ*, 25.

logical] here are peculiarly intertwined: the historical Jesus whose father and mother are well known (John 6:42) is at the same time supposed to be the preexistent Son of God, and alongside of the historical event of the cross stands the resurrection, which is not a historical event."[11]

Bultmann's point in all of this is that we live in a radically different—even incommensurable—cultural context from the authors of scripture, though this does not preclude intercultural communication since, like the kerygma itself, we are not reducible to our cultural situation. At the same time we cannot let the possibility of intercultural communication blind us to the cultural gulf that separates antiquity from modernity. The question for the church today is what it means to communicate the message of scripture for a modern audience: "There is no question that the New Testament represents the Christ occurrence as a mythical occurrence. The only question is whether it has to be thus represented or whether the New Testament itself provides us with a demythologizing interpretation."[12] Are we required to package the kerygma along with the ancient world-picture in which it was originally expressed, or can we translate the kerygma into a new world-picture? Bultmann argues for the latter, and he does so on the grounds that we already see demythologizing at work in the NT itself—specifically, in the different and even contradictory ways that the NT authors interpret what happened in Christ—as well as in the history of the church (consider the wide diversity in the interpretation of most biblical passages).

11. Bultmann, "New Testament," 32.
12. Ibid.

MYTH AS OBJECTIFYING THINKING

While Bultmann initially presented the need for demy-thologizing on the basis of the disparity in world-pictures, he later shifted the focus to the problem of what he calls "objectifying thinking" or simply "objectification." In making this shift he was actually returning to one of his earliest insights into the nature of myth. In 1927 he writes: "Myth speaks of God as that which transcends human beings, even though it speaks humanly of God."[13] The problem that Bultmann names as objectification concerns the way in which myth "speaks humanly" of God.

We have already touched on this theme above in our discussion of God's nonobjectifiability. Bultmann's discussion of myth has to be understood in connection with his writings on dialectical theology, where he explicates the transcendence and otherness of God. Recall that these writings were a criticism of the way liberal theology had turned God into an object of rational investigation and historical research. Bultmann's critique of mythology is an extension of this anti-liberal project. He finds in ancient mythology an innocent objectification of God that can lead to a pernicious objectification if not subjected to critical interpretation. In these ancient myths, God is described as a creaturely object and agent. The church fathers were well aware of the problem of biblical anthropomorphism and anthropopathism—the attribution of human characteristics, behaviors, and feelings to God—and Bultmann should be understood as a modern representative of this classical line of hermeneutical inquiry. Taking biblical mythology literally—as many of his conservative colleagues in the Confessing Church advocated—implies that God is little more than a glorified creature, which means that God

13. Bultmann, *Theologie als Kritik*, 214.

is intrinsically objectifiable. Biblical literalism thus leads to theological liberalism! And both lead to idolatry.

Bultmann articulates this position most forcefully in a 1952 essay written to clarify his program of demythologizing in response to widespread criticism, especially by church leaders in Germany who had put Bultmann on trial for heresy. This essay is one of the clearest and most comprehensive statements of his later hermeneutical theology. He reiterates his belief in the revelatory truth contained in myth, which he refers to as myth's "real intention." Myth, he says, "knows of another reality than the reality of the world that science has in view. It knows that the world and human life have their ground and limit in a power that lies beyond everything falling within the realm of human reckoning and control—in a transcendent power."[14] Myth in its essence is opposed to the objectification of God; it seeks to describe a truly transcendent reality. And yet, because of the limitations of its world-picture, it can only do so in language that is misleading.

> Myth talks about this transcendent reality and power inadequately when it represents the transcendent as spatially distant, as heaven above the earth, or as hell beneath it. It talks about the transcendent powers inadequately when it represents them as analogous to immanent powers and as superior to these powers only in force and unpredictability. . . . Myth talks about gods as human beings, and about their actions as human actions, with the difference that the gods are represented as endowed with superhuman power and their actions as unpredictable and able to break through the natural run of things. Myth thus makes the gods (or God) into human beings with superior power, and it does this even

14. Bultmann, "On the Problem," 98.

> when it speaks of God's omnipotence and om-
> niscience, because it does not distinguish these
> qualitatively from human power and knowledge
> but only quantitatively.[15]

To put it another way, myth is "a mode of thinking and speak-ing that objectifies the unworldly as something worldly."[16] Myth speaks about God inadequately by portraying God as only *quantitatively* superior to human beings—acting with greater power and unpredictability—and not as *quali-tatively* superior, as a genuinely transcendent God would necessarily be. Whereas liberal theology intentionally de-nies a qualitative superiority under the assumption that all things, including God, must be accessible to scientific analysis, ancient mythology unintentionally denies qualita-tive superiority in the effort to describe God's saving and revealing action in the world. The classic example of this is the miracle story in which God is portrayed as acting with superhuman power—most commonly, the power to heal—suggesting that God is an agent who has to intervene within the cosmic order like the *deus ex machina* of Greek tragedy. The God of the traditional miracle stories seems more like the fairy godmothers and action superheroes of modern mythology than the transcendent Lord confessed by the Christian faith.

There is, of course, much more to say about Bult-mann's project of demythologizing. The key here is to see that the criticism of mythology (a) is not the rejection of myth as such and (b) is an extension of his dialectical theol-ogy, with its concern for knowing God "according to faith (or the Spirit)" rather than "according to the flesh." Myth knows God according to faith, but it speaks according to the flesh. In our present world-picture, taking myth's manner of

15. Ibid., 98–99.

16. Bultmann, "On the Concept of 'Myth,'" 853.

speaking literally threatens to result in both speaking and knowing God according to the flesh. Bultmann subjects mythology to hermeneutical critique in an effort to ensure that we know God according to faith alone and thus as the God who savingly acted in Christ.

QUESTIONS FOR REFLECTION

1. Bultmann's concept of myth has been the subject of heated debate. What does the term "myth" or "mythology" evoke for you? Where do you see mythology in the world today?

2. What are the characteristics of the modern world-picture and where are some places we see it active? Are there other features of the modern world-picture besides the ones that Bultmann identifies that you would lift up as of greater importance?

3. What stands out to you as making it particularly difficult to see the ancient and modern world-pictures as compatible?

4. Has this connection between literalism and liberalism occurred to you before? Does it help make sense of your experience of contemporary Christianity?

5. What is your favorite miracle story in the Bible? If the popular conception of God as capable of working miracles in nature is not essential to faith, how could we interpret this miracle so that it does not objectify God as a merely superhuman agent?

8

HERMENEUTICS

THE PROBLEM OF HERMENEUTICS

HERMENEUTICS IS THE SCIENCE of interpretation, what Friedrich Schleiermacher calls "the art of understanding."[1] The effort to understand something, such as a text or person, is a hermeneutical endeavor. For Rudolf Bultmann, whose collected essays are appropriately titled *Faith and Understanding* (*Glauben und Verstehen*), hermeneutics is inherent in the theological task. Theology is concerned first and foremost with the interpretation of the biblical text, and like every text, the meaning of the scriptures is not self-evident. The reader cannot glean the meaning directly from the words on the page. The Bible's "sense," according to Francis Watson, "is a matter not only of passive reception but also of active construction. . . . The question is what principles or guidelines are to be followed in the act of interpretation."[2]

---

1. Schleiermacher, *Hermeneutics*, §1, 5.
2. Watson, "Hermeneutics," 118.

It is precisely the *active* nature of hermeneutics that makes it a "problem" many find threatening to faith. Gerhard Ebeling observes that "the Reformation conferred on the problem of hermeneutics a significance which, in spite of Origen and Augustine, it had never attained before."[3] And that is because the Roman Catholic doctrine of tradition addressed the hermeneutical task by precluding it. The authoritative tradition determines in advance what the meaning of scripture is. The work of "active construction" is removed from the hands of individual Christians, who are required instead to accept passively the teachings of the church. The Reformation, along with the vernacular translation of the Bible, exploded this arrangement and made the hermeneutical problem central to the life of faith. Protestants, of course, have had their own way of defusing the need for hermeneutics. The doctrine of verbal plenary inspiration, later known as inerrancy, was developed in the period of Protestant scholasticism and served the same purpose as the Catholic doctrine of tradition. Whereas the Catholics located the meaning of the text in the teaching authority of the church, Protestant orthodoxy located the meaning in the text itself. In both cases the meaning is presumed to be universal, timeless, and objectively self-evident. It is free from the contingencies of culture and history, immune to the perceived threats of scientific research and historical scholarship. In this way both Catholics and Protestants were able to shore up their authority and power in the face of the arrival of modernity.

Bultmann embraces the problem of hermeneutics for two reasons. The first is that it is unavoidable. He sees the challenge posed by what is known as "historical consciousness"—meaning the recognition that each person is not only situated within a particular historical situation but

3. Ebeling, "Word of God," 305.

is also an active participant in the formation of meaning within history—not as a threat but as a basic fact of life; it has always been the case even if it went unrecognized due to past cultural blinders. Every interpretation involves the subjectivity of the interpreter whether we like it or not. Indeed, for Bultmann the subjective aspect is what makes interpretation possible in the first place: "Only those are able to understand history who are themselves moved by sharing in history, that is, who are open to the language of history by their own responsibilities for the future. In this sense it is precisely the 'most subjective' interpretation of history that is the 'most objective.'"[4]

The second and more important reason for embracing hermeneutics, however, is that Bultmann sees it as the natural extension and outgrowth of Christian faith. Indeed, the rise of historical consciousness and the corresponding problem of hermeneutics is intrinsic to the theological revolution accomplished in the Reformation. Ebeling argues that the historical-critical method "has essentially a deep inner connexion with the Reformers' doctrine of justification," and that the decision in favor of the Protestant *sola fide* is a decision in favor of historical criticism.[5] The struggle against securing salvation through good works leads appropriately to a struggle against securing revelation through historical proofs. As we saw above in chapter 3, the doctrine of *sola fide* destroys every attempt to gain security outside of faith. This is why Bultmann claims that "radical demythologizing is the parallel to the Pauline-Lutheran doctrine of justification through faith alone without the works of the law."[6] The destabilizing nature of the hermeneutical task frees us from the illusion that salvation is

4. Bultmann, "Science," 138–39.

5. Ebeling, "Significance," 55.

6. Bultmann, "On the Problem," 122.

something we can possess. For Bultmann, the very reason hermeneutics is perceived by many to be a threat is the reason it is appropriate to Christian faith.

The theological basis for the problem of hermeneutics goes still deeper for Bultmann. It originates in the conviction that God is eschatologically transcendent. God is "wholly other," he argues, as the one who brings about the eschatological age in Jesus Christ. God is the God of the *future*, and is just as ungraspable and uncontrollable.

> God does not stand still and does not put up with being made an object of observation. . . . God always remains beyond what has once been grasped, which means that the decision of faith is genuine only as actualized ever anew. . . . As the one who demands my decision ever anew, God ever stands before me as one who is coming, and this constant futurity of God is God's transcendence.[7]

The problem of hermeneutics thus has its basis in the very nature of God. Since God is never static, always in movement, always encountering us anew, it follows that revelation, the word of God, is also always in movement. And that means the task of interpretation has to be carried out ever anew. The meaning of scripture—assuming that scripture in some sense mediates the revelation of God—does not stand still any more than God does. This means we need a hermeneutical method that is sensitive to the constant futurity of God. Bultmann finds such a method in what he calls "content criticism" (*Sachkritik*).

7. Bultmann, "Science," 144.

CONTENT CRITICISM

In order to understand Bultmann's hermeneutical method we first have to understand what he takes to be the goal of biblical interpretation. He does not see *description* of the biblical text as sufficient, for the same reason that historical research is not sufficient. To stop there would be like describing the human genome and concluding that one has defined what it means to be a human person. Or it would be like explaining how one's heart rate speeds up when in proximity to a person of interest and concluding that one has defined love. The problem is a reduction of some reality to empirical phenomena. For Bultmann, one cannot claim to have *interpreted* scripture unless one has engaged and understood "the subject matter [or content; *die Sache*] with which the text is concerned."[8] This of course means that "a particular understanding of the subject matter of the text . . . is always presupposed by exegesis," which is why exegesis is never presuppositionless.[9] Bultmann, for his part, presupposes that the subject matter of scripture is the kerygma.

Biblical hermeneutics, as Bultmann understands it, is a quest for the kerygma. Whereas the quest for the historical Jesus searched for a fixed empirical fact that could be objectively observed and analyzed, the kerygma as word-event proclaims a liberating, soteriological reality in Christ. By definition this is not something that can be contained in words; it is an existential event that personally involves the hearer. The personal involvement is not a *consequence* of the kerygma; it *is* the kerygma. To hear the kerygma means to encounter Christ's demand upon one's life and to respond obediently. This means that, while Bultmann believes the text bears witness to the kerygma,

8. Bultmann, "Is Exegesis Without Presuppositions," 145.
9. Ibid., 149.

we cannot point to a particular verse or passage as a *direct* representation of the kerygma. Instead, the interpretive task is to clarify and translate the text so that the message confronts us *as* the kerygma, that is, with its full kerygmatic force. Carrying out this task therefore requires *criticism* of the text, where the historical-cultural context obscures its purpose to bear witness to the kerygma. He calls this "content criticism" or "content exegesis," meaning an exegesis or criticism carried out in service of the "content" or "subject matter" of scripture.

In one of his earliest hermeneutical writings, written in 1925, Bultmann says that content exegesis or *Sachexegese* "seeks to perceive the light that shines through from beyond the surface [of the text], believing that this is the only way to understand what is meant." In other words, "the point of content exegesis is to know what *contents* [*Sachen*] are intended by the textual statements."[10] Here we see the antecedent to his later concept of myth's "real intention," and as with that later notion the point here is to say that the text, like myth, speaks to something beyond its own limited horizon. In content exegesis the assumption is that the meaning of the text is not "exhausted in the historically fixable, relative moment."[11] Bultmann presupposes that the biblical text "intends to refer to something outside the speaker, to disclose this to the hearer, and by so doing to become an *event* for the hearer." For this to happen, though, "*content criticism* of the text is both possible and necessary, namely, a criticism that differentiates between what is said and what is meant and measures what is said by its meaning."[12] Whereas other forms of criticism focus on issues like internal logic or historical data, content criticism

10. Bultmann, "Problem of a Theological Exegesis," 240, rev.

11. Ibid., rev.

12. Ibid., 241, rev.

assesses the text according to the criterion of the kerygma that is the ultimate object of the textual witness.

Bultmann's later hermeneutics, famously expressed in his program of demythologizing, is merely the extension of his early method of *Sachexegese*. In one of the many essays he wrote responding to critiques of his demythologizing program, he says: "In view of the differences existing within the NT it seems to me that a content criticism is inevitable, a criticism that has as its criterion the decisive basic idea of the NT, or perhaps better, the intention of the message resounding in the NT (Luther: 'what promotes Christ')."[13] What changes in Bultmann's later work is the recognition that it is the *mythical* nature of the text—understanding myth as a distinct mode of objectifying God-talk belonging to an ancient world-picture—that obscures one's ability to hear the NT's "decisive basic idea." Whether one accepts Bultmann's understanding of myth or not, the more decisive question is whether one accepts the method of content criticism. And that rests in turn on whether one believes that the text, despite its fallible, historically limited nature, witnesses to a revelatory truth beyond itself, in which case it is incumbent upon the interpreter to subject the text to faithful critique where this truth has been obfuscated.

As noted above, Bultmann's program of *Sachkritik* is a modern continuation and radicalization of Martin Luther's claim, which was made in the context of the latter's critique of the book of James, that only "what promotes Christ" (*was Christum treibet*) is truly faithful to the apostolic testimony.[14] Bultmann makes this connection to Luther explicit in the 1950 essay that he added as the epilogue to his *Theology of the New Testament*. He says, first, that "the theological thoughts of the New Testament can be normative only

13. Bultmann, "In eigener Sache," 186.
14. *LW*, 35:395–99.

insofar as they lead believers to develop out of their faith an understanding of God, the world, and human beings in their own concrete situation."[15] This is another way of saying that the NT is normative insofar as it facilitates an encounter with Christ. He then says that certain statements are more or less capable of facilitating this encounter. Some texts are clearer than others. Some texts speaks in terms that are inappropriate to the subject matter. "From this possibility," he adds, "arises the task—even in the case of the New Testament writings—of *content criticism* (Sachkritik) such as Luther, for example, exercised toward the Epistle of James and the Revelation of John."[16] Like Luther, Bultmann evaluates the biblical writings according to whether they confront a person with the gospel of Christ, and sometimes that leads to the conclusion that certain statements, perhaps certain books, are less authoritative than others, even at times contrary to the kerygma.

EXISTENTIALIST INTERPRETATION

Bultmann, of course, does not engage only in criticism. His hermeneutic is not merely negative; it is positive as well. The other side of demythologizing is what he calls "existentialist interpretation." The two sides are inseparable from each other: "Negatively, demythologizing is criticism of the mythical world picture insofar as it conceals the real intention of myth. Positively, demythologizing is existentialist

15. *TNT*, 2:238, rev. It is important to observe that Bultmann is not reductionist in his understanding of the object of faith. While the kerygmatic Christ is the ground and norm of theological knowledge, the believer comes to an understanding *of God, the world, and humankind.*

16. Ibid. One does not need to agree with Luther's assessment of James and Revelation to engage in content criticism; the point is the method, not the application.

interpretation, in that it seeks to make clear the intention of myth to talk about human existence."[17]

What does it mean to "talk about human existence"? One clue comes in the parallel between the negative and positive claims. We have already seen what he means by the "real intention of myth." For Bultmann that refers to the kerygmatic *Sache*, the soteriological subject matter of the text. The positive claim clarifies this further by defining myth's intention as the intention to talk about human existence. Many have assumed he means that the text does not tell us anything about God, that it only speaks about ourselves. But this fails to read Bultmann's statement charitably and in context. If we interpret "human existence" in terms of myth's "real intention," we arrive at a better understanding. To speak about human existence is to speak about the kerygma, which makes sense, since the kerygma for Bultmann is not something objectively "out there" that we can observe from a safe, neutral distance. The kerygma is rather the event of God's self-involving word to us, and to hear this word is by definition to be caught up in it, to hear God's gracious judgment and justification. The task of uncovering and understanding the "real intention" of the text entails understanding *ourselves* as those addressed by God. We thus speak about the kerygma by speaking at the same time of human existence. For this reason, after citing Melanchthon's famous dictum, "to know Christ is to know his benefits," Bultmann adds: "Such interpretation . . . is existentialist interpretation."[18]

First and foremost, therefore, existentialist interpretation means interpretation that discloses the *existential significance* of the text's subject matter. In order to disclose this significance, however, Bultmann believes that the text

17. Bultmann, "On the Problem," 99.
18. Ibid.

must be *translated* into the conceptual idiom of the present hearers. The act of translation goes hand-in-hand with the task of criticism. The biblical texts "speak in a strange language, in concepts of a faraway time, of a world picture that is alien to us," and for this reason "they must be *translated*."[19] They can only be truly understood, in other words, if their content is recontextualized within the cultural situation of those encountering the text today. The biblical text contains contextualizations of the kerygma for various ancient audiences, especially those of the ancient Near East and Hellenistic Judaism. These contexts or world-pictures presuppose the naturalness of certain ideas, concepts, and behaviors that condition how the kerygma is received and understood. The kerygma's intrinsic flexibility means it is able to inhabit and embrace an infinite variety of contexts, while always presenting a challenge to every context by virtue of the way it liberates us from our sinful past and calls us to a new life of obedience. This cultural flexibility is what enables Christianity's history of ongoing contextualization. Bultmann's work is an exercise in translation for his situation and within that context he found the existentialist conceptuality of Heidegger to be the most fruitful for fulfilling the task of interpretation, though it is by no means the only conceptuality one can use. Indeed, he was convinced that "even the most accurate translation itself needs to be translated in the next generation," and this means one will likely need to adopt a new conceptuality appropriate for a new situation.[20]

One of the concepts Bultmann appropriates is one we already examined above in the chapter on nonobjectifiability, namely, the concept of *Vorhandenheit* or "objective presence." As we saw in that discussion, the term comes

19. Bultmann, "Is Exegesis Without Presuppositions," 148.

20. Bultmann, "Theology as Science," 59.

with a prior history of use by Heidegger, but Bultmann appropriates it within his theological-exegetical interpretation of the Pauline notion of flesh (*sarx*) and the Johannine notion of world (*kosmos*). The most important concept that Bultmann appropriates is *Eigentlichkeit* or "authenticity," which Bultmann uses as an existentialist translation for the biblical idea of salvation. Bultmann still speaks often of salvation, since he does not want to lose the important connotations of that word, but he finds authenticity helpful as a way of communicating the meaning of the kerygma to contemporary people. Specifically, it helps to emphasize the fact that salvation is not about a person's destination after death but concerns the mode of one's life here and now. One can either live authentically (i.e., in obedience to God) or inauthentically (i.e., in disobedience). Responding to the kerygma in faith, a possibility that "is—in traditional terminology—the work of the Holy Spirit," means that one makes the radical decision to live authentically.[21]

In the case of every concept Bultmann appropriates for the task of interpretation, the word is used in a purely formal sense. The word "authenticity" does not come prepackaged with a definite understanding of what it means to live authentically. This addresses a central objection to Bultmann's positive program:

> There would be reason to object at this point only if the concept of the authenticity of existence developed by philosophy were thought to be a material ideal of existence—in other words, if philosophy were to prescribe to us: *so* should you exist! But philosophy says to us only: you should *exist!* Or if that is already to say too much, philosophy shows us what existing means. It shows us that human being, in contradistinction

21. Bultmann, "On the Problem," 106.

> from all other being, means precisely to exist—
> to be a being that is given over to itself and has
> to take responsibility for itself.[22]

Existentialist philosophy only says what Bultmann already knows on the basis of the NT, namely, that each person is responsible for her or his own life. What philosophy cannot say is what that responsibility actually involves. Like other philosophers, Heidegger believes that each person has the inherent ability to exist authentically. "Philosophy is convinced that all that is needed to bring about the realization of our 'nature' is that it be shown to us," and yet here we see "its difference from the New Testament, which claims that we can in no way free ourselves from our factual fallenness in the world but are freed from it only by an act of God."[23] And not just any act of God but specifically the "liberating act of God . . . that is realized in Christ."[24] It is *this* event of liberation that Bultmann describes using Heidegger's language of authenticity. The *material content* of the word in Bultmann's exegetical translations is thus determined by his prior understanding of the subject matter, namely, the kerygma that proclaims and actualizes the eschatological event. Put another way, the existentialist conceptuality (philosophy) is entirely in service to the text's existential significance (kerygma). As the norm for all translation, the kerygma determines which philosophy is most appropriate for the hermeneutical task and what the concepts mean in the context of the interpretation.[25]

22. Ibid., 107.

23. Bultmann, "New Testament," 25–26.

24. Ibid., 26.

25. When Bultmann writes that "Martin Heidegger's existentialist analysis of human existence seems to be only a profane philosophical presentation of the New Testament view of who we are" (Bultmann, "New Testament," 23), he is not assuming the correctness of

TRANSLATION AND CONCORDISM

We must keep in mind this emphasis on the kerygmatic norm in order to distinguish Bultmann's program from certain contemporary distortions of the task of translation. An example of such distortion is found in the American evangelical debate over the relationship between Christianity and science. The dispute revolves around the issue of what is known as *concordism*, which in this context "refers to a method of biblical interpretation that seeks to find a correspondence between science and Scripture."[26] The concordists believe that the Bible makes scientific claims that correspond to, and sometimes compete with, what modern science knows about the cosmos.[27] For example, old earth creationist Hugh Ross claims that the frequent description of the heavens as "stretched out" like a curtain or tent (e.g., Job 9:8; Ps 104:2; Isa 40:22) is "identical to the big bang concept of cosmic expansion," and the statement that YHWH "founded the earth" (Zech 12:1) is "consistent with the geophysical discovery that certain long-lived radiometric elements were placed into the earth's crust a little more than four billion years ago in just the right quantities."[28]

Heidegger's philosophy and then simply conforming his understanding of the NT to fit Heidegger. On the contrary, he finds in Heidegger a philosophical articulation of something he has already found in the NT. What impressed him about Heidegger's work was the way it cohered with his reading of the NT, at least within certain limits.

26. Lamoureux, *Evolutionary Creation*, 14.

27. The so-called "old earth creationists" (Reasons to Believe) generally find points of correspondence, whereas the "young earth creationists" (Answers in Genesis, Institute of Creation Research) generally find points of conflict. Both groups conflict with the scientific consensus on human origins. The so-called "evolutionary creationists" (BioLogos) reject scientific concordism altogether.

28. Ross, *Creator*, 25.

The Old Testament scholar John Walton criticizes concordism as an "attempt to 'translate' the culture and text for the modern reader. The problem is, we cannot translate their cosmology to our cosmology, nor should we."[29] A concordist interpretation "intentionally attempts to read an ancient text in modern terms. . . . Such interpretation does not represent in any way what the biblical author would have intended or what the audience would have understood. Instead it gives modern meaning to ancient words."[30] Walton objects to concordism on the grounds that it seeks to translate the meaning of the text from its ancient culture to our modern one. Any attempt to find a modern, contemporary meaning in the ancient words is ruled out in principle. He makes this explicit in the introduction where he calls cultural translation—as opposed to the mere linguistic translation of an ancient word to a modern word—"an imperialistic act" that involves "taking [a word] out of its context and fitting it into ours."[31] Walton advocates a method of *interpretation without translation* in which the reader "must make every attempt to set our English categories aside, to leave our cultural ideas behind, and try our best (as limited as the attempt might be) to understand the material in its cultural context without translating it."[32]

Laudable as Walton's rejection of naïve creationist concordism may be, his hermeneutical approach throws the baby out with the bathwater. By rejecting all cultural translation, he confines the meaning of the biblical text to the "author's intention" and assumes we are able to reconstruct this intention by understanding its ancient cultural context. Even if we were to grant that the intention

29. Walton, *Lost World*, 15.
30. Ibid., 103–4.
31. Ibid., 8.
32. Ibid., 9.

of the original author could be accessed through historical research, it does not follow that all cultural translation is imperialism. The underlying assumption here is a conflation between divine revelation and the text as a cultural-historical artifact. Walton presupposes that the text itself *is* God's revelation, and the only question then is whether the text speaks within its limited cultural horizon or whether God inspired it to speak to the modern scientific age. What Walton lacks is a theologically nuanced distinction between scripture and revelation—between the biblical text and the kerygmatic norm—that would allow for a program of content criticism as well as ongoing hermeneutical translation.

Denis Lamoureux proves helpful at this point. He distinguishes between three different kinds of concordism: (1) "cosmological concordism" (or "scientific concordism") posits a correspondence between the biblical text and modern scientific accounts of the origin and nature of the cosmos; (2) "historical concordism" asserts that the Bible is a historically accurate document with respect to certain periods of history whose claims can be verified by archaeological evidence; and (3) "theological concordism" (or "spiritual concordism"), which Lamoureux calls the "most important type," states that there is a correspondence between the theological truths of scripture and the "spiritual realities we experience in our lives."[33] The fundamentalist creationists insist on all three types of concordism, though to varying extents. Most evangelical scholars, including Walton, hold to types 2 and 3, though if we understand theological concordism to include the possibility in principle of theological *translation* from one cultural context to another, then it would seem Walton only accepts type 2. For his part, Bultmann does not reject type 2 altogether—a common

33. See Lamoureux, "Evangelicals," 38n79; Lamoureux, *Evolutionary Creation*, 14–16.

misperception—but he certainly makes it as minimal as possible; the lion's share of his interest is in type 3 as the basis for the critical work of interpretation and translation.

What separates theological concordism from the other two types is its nonempirical character. Whereas scientific and historical concordism connect scripture to the world in ways that are objectively accessible apart from faith, theological concordism finds a connection between scripture and faith, that is, between the claim of the text and the existence of the reader. Put another way, theological concordism implies a norm that transcends the text, along with every cultural context, and is thus capable of connecting the ancient text and contemporary interpreters. For Bultmann that norm is the kerygma. By contrast, both scientific concordists like Ross and nonconcordists like Walton lack any such norm, or rather, they make the text itself the norm. The result is that the concordists are unable to acknowledge the culturally alien nature of the text, while the nonconcordists are unable to acknowledge a transcultural norm to which the text bears witness. Bultmann's historical work aims to show that the scriptures "speak in a strange language, in concepts of a faraway time, of a world picture that is alien to us," but this does not preclude the possibility of the text speaking to us today via translation in our own language, in contemporary concepts, in a world-picture that is familiar to us.[34] Indeed, if we are to hear and respond to its claim upon our lives, then it *must* speak to us in this way.

QUESTIONS FOR DISCUSSION

1. What is the understanding of the kerygma (or norm) that you presuppose in your interpretation of scripture? How is it different from Bultmann's kerygma?

34. Bultmann, "Is Exegesis Without Presuppositions," 148.

2. Bultmann and Ebeling approached hermeneutics from within their German Lutheran context. How might the problem of hermeneutics look differently if we approach it from a global, pluralistic perspective that takes into consideration the reality of world Christianity? What would the *intercultural* problem of hermeneutics mean for the interpretation of scripture?

3. Is it possible and/or desirable to interpret the Bible without having a "canon within the canon"? Why or why not?

4. If Bultmann were alive today, which philosophical conceptuality might he appropriate for the task of translation? Are there certain philosophies that we should not appropriate? If so, which ones and why?

5. Are there other types of concordism besides the three that Lamoureux mentions? How legitimate are they?

6. The past two decades have seen the rise of what is called the "theological interpretation of scripture" (TIS). How is TIS similar to and different from Bultmann's content criticism? What is the relationship between TIS's rule of faith (*regula fidei*) and Bultmann's kerygma?

9

FREEDOM

HUMANISM IN POST-WAR GERMANY

"WHEN THE ALLIES . . . finally marched in, I, along with many friends, greeted the end of Nazi rule as a liberation."[1] So wrote Bultmann in his autobiographical reflections of 1956. He observes that, during the era of Nazi rule, "life in the university and in society at large was poisoned by mistrust and denunciations. Only within a small circle of like-minded acquaintances could one enjoy the open and invigorating exchange of the intellectual world." At the University of Marburg, he and Hans von Soden spurned the Nazi officials and "endeavored to see that free scholarly work retained its proper place."[2] It is thus appropriate that, following their liberation, Bultmann was actively involved in the denazification of the academy. He was a member of the committee that oversaw the reform of German schools, and he protested against the reinstatement of professors

1. Bultmann, "Autobiographical Reflections," xxi.
2. Ibid.

who had National Socialist sympathies.[3] In a letter to Günther Bornkamm on December 23, 1945, Bultmann decried a recent lecture by Hans Asmussen on humanism and Christianity, which criticized the Allies "in the style of National Socialist propaganda, and which naturally captivated the students due to its rigid dogmatism."[4]

The topic of humanism and Christianity touched a nerve for Bultmann. The years following the Second World War were a time of reckoning and reflection, and like many German intellectuals of his day, Bultmann wanted to understand what had happened and how they had arrived at that point. His conclusion in part revolved around this topic of humanism. There were multiple facets to the problem. With respect to the reconstruction and denazification of Germany, Bultmann sought to reinstate a classical humanism that the Nazi regime had tried their best to smother. Lisa Pine, in her work on education within Nazi Germany, summarizes the matter well:

> Overall, the Nazi leadership disliked and distrusted the *Gymnasium* [the elite secondary school system in Germany] with its humanist tradition, its emphasis on classical education and its academic snobbery. Historically, the *Gymnasium* emerged in the tradition of classical humanism.... The Nazi government aimed both to decrease the significance of the *Gymnasium* and to reduce the influence of the Churches in German education.[5]

3. Standhartinger, "Bultmann's *Theology*," 244.

4. Bultmann and Bornkamm, *Briefwechsel 1926–1976*, 161. It should be noted that Asmussen himself was a friend and supporter of the Confessing Church, but this particular lecture aroused and inspired Nazi supporters in the audience.

5. Pine, *Education*, 138.

Even though the Third Reich fell in 1945, young people in Germany "still clung to some of the 'values' inculcated through education under National Socialism, and found some degree of refuge in the rigid dogmas of the church."[6] In response to the loss of classical education, Bultmann called for the mandatory study of classical antiquity. He was of the opinion that the connection between the university and antiquity, especially Socratic and Platonic philosophy, "must be returned to consciousness in order to counter the National Socialists' misuse of knowledge. . . . The study of antiquity . . . exposed all the fundamental problems of human life."[7] Knowledge of the ancient past does not provide us with the solutions to our problems but helps us to think critically about them.

Despite the antihumanist aims of Nazi policies, Bultmann was keenly aware that many people in Germany, particularly those associated with the church, blamed the tradition of humanism—understood as belief in the dignity, responsibility, and freedom of humankind—for causing this mess in the first place. He responded to this claim in various essays. Two in particular, both titled "Humanism and Christianity," are worth noting. In the first, published in 1948, he says that "if humanism has been held responsible for this [i.e., the relativism and nihilism of the twentieth century]—and that has repeatedly happened unfortunately from the church's side—that rests on a fundamental misunderstanding." Humanism's belief in human dignity and autonomy does not mean that it endorses the "arbitrariness of subjectivism" over against the pursuit of truth, justice, the good, and the beautiful.[8] He reinforced this point in the later essay, which was a lecture he presented during

6. Hammann, *Rudolf Bultmann*, 375.

7. Standhartinger, "Bultmann's *Theology*," 245.

8. Bultmann, "Humanism [1948]," 165, rev.

his 1951 trip to the United States at Wellesley College, the University of Chicago, Emory University, and Union Theological Seminary in New York.[9] There he writes:

> When after the second World War our culture lay in ruins, and minds and hearts were moved to seek reasons for these catastrophes, the answer became louder and louder: Humanity's faith in itself is responsible; faith in human beings who recognize no divine power above themselves; faith in human beings who make their own law, who decide by themselves what is good and evil, who claim to be master of their fate. The catastrophes are God's judgment on human beings who have fallen victims to this delusion.[10]

Bultmann agreed that these were catastrophes, but he rejected the assertion that humanism, including the *Gymnasium* with which it was associated, was to blame. Indeed, he placed the blame on "a faith in the power and reason of human beings that is totally unhumanistic, that is presumption (*hybris*) indeed."[11]

The mistake made by the critics of humanism in postwar Germany was to assume that autonomy means freedom from all norms and constraints, which thus gives free reign to relativism and the arbitrary will of the individual. Since Christianity opposes this kind of voluntarism, these critics concluded that Christianity opposes humanism as such.

9. Bultmann and Bornkamm, *Briefwechsel* 1926–1976, 230, 239, 249, 253. Bultmann visited many other locations, of course, but these are the places he gave this particular lecture. Bultmann gave another lecture on this topic during the trip to the United States titled: "The Significance of the Idea of Freedom for Western Civilization" (*GuV*, 2:274–93; *Essays*, 305–25).

10. Bultmann, "Humanism [1952]," 79, rev.

11. Ibid., 80, rev.

At issue here is the nature of freedom in both humanism and Christianity. Bultmann rejected the crude dichotomy between humanism and Christianity, but he also denied that the two positions were in agreement on the nature of genuine freedom. The aim of these post-war writings is thus to clarify the concept of freedom, not only for the sake of Christian self-understanding but also for the healing and restoration of German society in the aftermath of its self-destruction.

THE FREEDOM OF THE CHRISTIAN

The "faith in humanity" that characterizes classical humanism, according to Bultmann, is "not at all faith in humanity in its empirical objective presence [*Vorfindlichkeit*], in its reason, in its right and ability to make the law for itself and for the world." Humanism instead is "faith in the idea of humanity that stands as a norm over concrete life," that is to say, "faith in the spirit in which humanity participates," which empowers human pursuit of the true, the good, and the beautiful.[12] Humanism affirms a transcendent, spiritual realm that serves as ideal and norm for human life. Individual freedom, according to Aristotle, is thus "constituted by the νόμος [law] of the πόλις [city], which maintains the law."[13] Autonomy is the freedom to realize this norm or law within concrete existence; it is not the arbitrary will of the individual. For humanism "there is genuine freedom only in the obligation to a norm superior to the subjective, arbitrary will."[14] Arbitrary, voluntaristic freedom is a "sham-freedom" (*Scheinfreiheit*) that is really only "dependence on what excites lust and passion in the moment. Genuine

12. Ibid., rev. Cf. *GuV*, 3:65.
13. Bultmann, "Significance of the Idea," 306.
14. Bultmann, "Humanism [1952]," 81, rev.

freedom is precisely freedom from the motivation of the moment. . . . Freedom is obedience to that law whose truth and validity are recognized and to which consent is given, which one recognizes as the law of one's own being, as the law of the spirit."[15]

Thus far Bultmann wants to show that humanism and Christianity are allies in the struggle to oppose the arbitrary will-to-power that characterized the Nazi regime. Bultmann promotes the study of antiquity not only because it sharpens one's critical thinking but also because it affirms the kind of ethical norms that society needs to avoid further catastrophes. Unlike many classical Christian thinkers, however, Bultmann does not find any straightforward continuity between the ancient Greek norms of truth, goodness, and beauty and Christian faith. And that is because "the world of the spirit is a part of that world which God brings to an end and from which God frees people."[16] Whereas humanism posits an immanent ideal toward which human beings can strive through a gradual process of cultural labor, Christianity posits a transcendent, "wholly other" norm—the "constant futurity" of God's transcendence—that places the entirety of our worldly life in question and calls us "to enter the darkness of the future hopefully and confidently."[17] Of course, this hardly means Christianity rejects the norms of truth, goodness, and beauty. Bultmann is willing to call these the law of God, so that humanism and Christianity relate to one another as law and gospel.[18] But whereas Greek humanism claims that the law can be fulfilled by human resolve, "the Christian

15. Ibid., rev. Cf. Bultmann, "Significance of the Idea," 307.

16. Bultmann, "Humanism [1952]," 82, rev.

17. Ibid., 83.

18. Bultmann, "Humanism [1948]," 166. On the unique way in which Bultmann relates law and gospel, see Congdon, *Mission*, 52–69.

faith says that this is indeed impossible without the grace of God."[19]

Here we arrive at what Bultmann calls the "either-or" between humanism and Christianity: where humanism assumes that people have the freedom to actualize their spiritual ideals and norms, Christianity claims that people do not have this freedom. Indeed, not only do people lack this freedom; they are actually in revolt against God and so live in bondage to the past, to themselves. The only way to become truly free is to be "freed from themselves—that is, from the selves that they have previously made of themselves, from their past that ties them down, or in Christian terms: from their sin."[20] Freedom is not something we possess but something we *receive* in our encounter with God.

We can further clarify the Christian understanding of freedom by differentiating it from gnostic and stoic conceptions of freedom. As Bultmann understands it,[21] gnosticism posits a cosmological dualism between two groups of people, those of God or the light and those of the world or the darkness, and each person is determined from the outset by the group or nature into which one is born. Those who belong to the light are freed from the world in a static, nondialectical dualism of nature.[22] The Gospel of John, by contrast, replaces the dualism of nature with a "dualism of decision," in which belonging to God or the world is not a

---

19. Bultmann, "Humanism [1952]," 84.

20. Bultmann, "Significance of the Idea," 309, rev. Cf. *GuV*, 2:278.

21. Since gnosticism likely developed only after the origin of Christianity, we can no longer accept Bultmann's historical claim that early Christianity was in critical dialogue with gnostic beliefs. Nevertheless, the category of gnosticism remains permanently useful as a foil for Bultmann's articulation of Christian theology.

22. *TNT*, 2:21.

matter of fate or nature but of personal response to God.[23] In faith, which is a divine gift, one decides for God against the world, but one is not thereby removed from the world; one is freed *from* the world while remaining simultaneously *in* the world—indeed, faith frees us *for* the world.[24] Christian freedom in this sense is always dialectical; it has to be exercised, by God's liberating grace, ever anew, and it is exercised always within our worldly, historical situation.

Like stoicism, Christianity proposes a primarily inner, spiritual freedom. But here, too, there is a sharp distinction between the two accounts. Stoicism understands human freedom as an inner *security* rooted in the exercise of reason. Christianity understands freedom, rather, as an inner *insecurity* rooted in the gift of divine grace. The stoic pursuit of security "is never attainable for the Christian, who is subject to the incontrollable law of grace; for grace can never be possessed, but can only be received afresh again and again." Indeed, for the Christian, "insecurity and radical freedom [are] identical," since "freedom . . . is not a *quality*, but can only be an *event* at any given time."[25] Freedom, in other words, is an eschatological and nonobjectifiable occurrence. It comes to us from the future and beckons us into it—a future that demands we abandon the possessions and securities to which we desperately cling in self-preservation.

23. *TNT*, 2:76.

24. Bultmann's term for this is *Entweltlichung*, translated best as "deworldlizing." The similarity of *Entweltlichung* to *Entmythologisierung* (demythologizing) is intentional and important, but both words give the unfortunate impression of being one-sidedly negative: *against* myth and *against* the world. In truth, both words have to be understood dialectically: demythologizing frees us from myth only by affirming myth's real intention; deworldlizing frees us from the world only by placing us more fully in the world.

25. Bultmann, "Significance of the Idea," 310.

The fact that freedom is an event of divine grace means that, in contrast to Hellenism, the law cannot establish freedom. But this does not mean the law is entirely abolished. "Rather one could say, conversely, that according to Paul, freedom establishes the law."[26] The notion of the law as something that "limits freedom" and for that reason can be used "to secure fulfillment through it" has been abolished in Christ, and yet "its actual purpose of leading to life is thereby restored. For now it can be fulfilled in genuine obedience without the aim of securing oneself. Those who are liberated by grace from themselves are free to love." In this way, Bultmann says, "the law is therefore established by freedom."[27] Having been freed from the law as a means of gaining security, the Christian is freed *for* the law as a means of loving the neighbor in need.

THE FREEDOM OF THE CHURCH

Having lived through two world wars, Bultmann was deeply concerned about the future of western civilization. In 1952 he saw social and political developments, particularly the rise of the bureaucratic, technological state, as an especially great danger to human freedom.[28] Nevertheless, as a theologian of the church, Bultmann most frequently explored the implications this account of freedom has for the community of faith. His program of demythologizing, for instance, is rightly understood in this regard as a *hermeneutic of freedom*. He concluded his 1952 defense of this program with the claim that demythologizing "destroys every false security and every false demand for security, whether it is grounded on our good action or on our certain knowl-

26. Bultmann, "Gedanke," 49.

27. Ibid., 50.

28. Bultmann, "Significance of the Idea," 315.

edge. . . . They alone find security who let all security go, who—to speak with Luther—are ready to enter into inner darkness."[29] While God speaks through myth, the attempt to make the mythical forms of biblical discourse timeless and essential is an effort to establish a false security that gives us control over God's revelation. In this sense demythologizing clears aside the cultural barriers to the freedom of Christian faith.

Three years earlier Bultmann wrote a piece for the post-war journal *Die Wandlung*—a periodical launched in 1945 (lasting only until 1949) by leading German intellectuals to promote the spiritual renewal of German society—in which he defended the Hamburg pastor and theologian Erwin Gross, who put forward sharp criticisms of the Protestant church for the way "a false security is growing up in the church because a pietistic orthodoxy is at work to gain control."[30] Gross was criticized in a polemical article published in the periodical *Junge Kirche*, which Bultmann found ironically to be "a sad confirmation of [Gross's] thesis."[31] Bultmann goes on to summarize Gross's position as follows:

> He wants to fight for the genuine freedom of faith that he sees threatened—indeed, already abandoned—in the present development within the church. But what is this freedom? It is freedom by and for grace, and this means, at the same time, for the freedom of God. That is, it is release from all worldly conditions and radical openness for encounters with God in all that comes. Further, it is the renunciation of every security that a man might acquire by assent to

29. Bultmann, "On the Problem," 122.
30. Bultmann, "On Behalf of Christian Freedom," 96.
31. Ibid., 95.

"right doctrine" or by appropriate practical con-
duct; it is the renunciation of every "standpoint"
by which he could make the free grace of God
his possession. In other words, it is the renunciation of every "legalism"; for every such security
is a legalistic security. The genuine freedom of
faith is man's radical surrender to God's grace as
the sole means whereby he is saved from his factual insecurity, his total lostness. But this grace
"must necessarily appear to the man who lives in
legalism in the form of an offending, perplexing,
and frightening annihilation" (Gross, p. 710).
Thus freedom is the readiness to sink into the
"abyss of nothingness" (p. 708), or, to express the
matter with Luther, it is the readiness to go out
into utter darkness.[32]

All of Bultmann's key themes coalesce in this passage,
and the reference to Luther, in particular, forms a bridge
between his reflections on freedom and his hermeneutical
writings. In fact, while writing this article, Bultmann was
caught in the midst of a heated debate over the "orthodoxy"
of his own theology—a controversy that had begun in ear-
nest only the year before.[33] His defense of Gross is, in one
sense, an indirect defense of himself. Bultmann addresses
the issue of orthodox doctrine later in the essay. While he
acknowledges, in a correction of Gross, that "'pure doctrine'
must indeed be the constant concern of theological reflection," he adds that such doctrine can never be permanently
fixed since "pure doctrine" is an eschatological reality that
is always "standing before me in the future."[34] Pure, orthodox doctrine, if we can speak of such a thing, can only be
the kerygma—the eschatological word-event that stands

32. Ibid.
33. See Hammann, *Rudolf Bultmann*, 443–44.
34. Bultmann, "On Behalf of Christian Freedom," 97.

beyond all theological statements. For this reason, the truly orthodox theology is the one that abandons the security of a timeless theological system and follows God freely and fearlessly into the "utter darkness" of the future.

FREEDOM FROM THE PAST— FREEDOM FOR THE FUTURE

Bultmann's struggle for freedom is particularly relevant for those living in North America today. Socially, American society is the opposite of what Bultmann experienced in Germany; instead of a totalitarian fascism that subsumed individuals within the collective will of the nation, American society promotes, in the name of freedom, a relativistic individualism that is really a sham-freedom manifesting itself as enslavement to arbitrary passion. In the United States, correspondingly, we see a rapidly growing libertarian political movement that advocates an abstract, negative freedom from communal demands and government control. In response to this cultural phenomenon, many religious thinkers have (wrongly) placed the blame for this state of affairs on Enlightenment humanism with its doctrine of human autonomy. It is ironic that the same historical development is blamed for two completely opposite political positions—fascism and libertarianism. Bultmann's description of people in his own day applies just as well to critics of modernity in the United States: "Thus we are told that the only way out is to abandon idealism, humanism, the doctrine of the autonomy of humanity, and to return to Christianity, to theonomy."[35] Indeed, this is precisely what we hear on a regular basis today. But as Bultmann points out, "theonomy is either autonomy or heteronomy."[36] The

35. Bultmann, "Humanism [1952]," 79, rev.
36. Ibid., 81.

attempt to pit Christianity against modern autonomy ends up misconstruing both terms.

Bultmann's theology of freedom is even more relevant within theological discourse, where the rejection of modernity has become, in some circles, an indicator of one's orthodoxy. Embracing modernity within Christianity is now frequently tantamount to denying the deity of Christ. The ecclesial tides shifted in North America around the time of Bultmann's death in 1976.[37] Two years earlier, Hans Frei published his pioneering work, *The Eclipse of Biblical Narrative*, which launched a widespread turn away from the problem of hermeneutics that had consumed the Bultmann school toward a narrative or postliberal theology, which advocated a "plain" reading of the text that was more in keeping with premodern interpreters of scripture. This was followed by David Kelsey's *The Uses of Scripture in Recent Theology* in 1975, Thomas Oden's public turn from Bultmann to patristic theology in his 1979 book, *Agenda for Theology: Recovering Christian Roots*, and David Steinmetz's significant article on "The Superiority of Pre-Critical Exegesis" in 1980. Evangelicals had their own backlash against modernity during this time. The "Chicago Statement on Biblical Inerrancy" was drafted in 1978. The years since have for many only further bolstered the view that modernity was a "fall" in human history, and that it is our duty as Christians to recover the superior theology and exegesis of the ancient and medieval church. That this is taking place in the fields of systematic theology and biblical studies indicates how dramatic the sea change has been. Perhaps most emblematic of the new "orthodoxy" is the prominence of what is called theological interpretation of

37. This is hardly coincidental, of course, since many of these writers were responding directly to the controversies over Bultmann's theological program.

scripture, which typically involves reading the biblical text in terms of the *regula fidei* (rule of faith) as codified in the classical creeds and confessions of the church.

It is impossible to say for sure how Bultmann might have responded to these theological developments, but we find some clues in the writings we have considered above. Almost certainly he would have been troubled and perplexed by the way so many Protestants today are of the conviction that the answers to their theological, ecclesial, and sociopolitical dilemmas are to be found by returning to the ideas of some past period in church history, prior to the age of Enlightenment. Responding to similar views in his own day, Bultmann writes:

> Such repristination of a past stage of development is impossible. Genuine loyalty to tradition does not consist in the canonization of a particular stage in history. It is, of course, always criticism of the present before the tribunal of tradition; but it is also criticism of tradition before the tribunal of the present. Genuine loyalty is not repetition [*Wiederholung*] but rather continuation [*Weiterführung*].[38]

Theology in North America for the past two decades has been an age of repristination, repetition, and *ressourcement*—an attempt to counter modernity by returning to the resources of the past.[39] To be sure, Bultmann is not opposed to learning from the past. As he says elsewhere in the same essay, "freedom from the past does not result in a denial of the past, but in the positive appreciation of it."[40] The issue is not the appreciation of the past but its *canon-*

38. Bultmann, "Significance of the Idea," 315, rev.

39. For an overview of these various movements, see Buschart and Eilers, *Theology as Retrieval*.

40. Bultmann, "Significance of the Idea," 321.

ization, in which ancient tradition is set up as an infallible, universal norm for contemporary theological construction. Bultmann sees in such approaches "the kind of security that does not engage in discussion freely but rather seeks to hinder it by doctrinal discipline." A church clinging to this security "holds that every attack on the presently approved form of the church is a refusal of the church's claim. . . . Precisely when the church interprets every genuine opposition in this sense and thereby makes itself deaf to all criticism, it proves that it has fallen into the security that is the security of legalism and denies the freedom of God."[41]

The point is not that all efforts at retrieval and *ressourcement* are legalistic denials of God's freedom. There are many rich and lasting insights to be gained from the study of the church's past. One can even say that such study is a prerequisite for responsible theological reflection. Bultmann was a tireless advocate of the study of antiquity and insisted on historical research as the starting point for exegesis. But if tradition is not to become a kind of false security that prevents constructive dialogue, the church will have to understand itself as free from the past, and only in this way truly free *for* it. The church can only engage tradition appropriately if it does so without fear—whether fear of modernity, postmodernity, or whatever lies beyond the theological horizon—in a radical surrender to God's grace.

The problem with appeals to the *regula fidei* is the assumption that this "rule" is already fixed. The future becomes only the repeated application of this rule. Bultmann challenges us to consider the possibility that God's grace frees us for the ongoing development of the rule itself, and even for new rules, so to speak, that assist the translation of the kerygma in new times and places. If the freedom of God is "the readiness to go out into utter darkness," then

41. Bultmann, "On Behalf of Christian Freedom," 97.

no canon, creed, or confession is fixed once for all time. Instead, all of our theological statements must be tested anew before the eschatological tribunal of the kerygmatic Christ, whose word resists every objectification and calls us into the insecurity of God's future.[42]

QUESTIONS FOR REFLECTION

1. Responding to political developments in the mid-twentieth century, Bultmann says "there is room for the *renunciation of the security* to which modern life was accustomed. There must be a clear recognition of the fact that the greatest possible limitation of personal freedom goes along with the greatest possible security."[43] How might Bultmann respond to the Transportation Security Administration and National Security Agency in the United States, particularly in the wake of the Edward Snowden revelations?

2. Is it possible to develop a systematic theology on Bultmannian grounds? If so, what might it look like?

3. What is the difference between the *security* of orthodoxy and *assurance* of faith? Is it possible to affirm assurance without leading to security?

---

42. Bultmann is here quite close to Barth, who spoke toward the end of his career of the need for a "theology of freedom" (Barth, *Evangelical Theology*, xii). By this phrase, Daniel Migliore says, "Barth meant a theology free *from* all ideological straightjackets and deadening theological 'isms,' a theology free *for* the God of the gospel, who in free grace turns to humankind in Jesus Christ and whose continuing activity in the world in the power of his Spirit cannot be captured and imprisoned by old or new orthodoxies, whether ecclesiastical, philosophical, or sociopolitical" (Migliore, "*Veni Creator Spiritus*," 157–58).

43. Bultmann, "Significance of the Idea," 315.

4. What implications does Bultmann's defense of classical humanism have for theological education?

5. In light of what Bultmann says about God's grace establishing the law, how should we situate him in relation to the Reformed and Lutheran debates over the relation between law and gospel?

10

ADVENT

BULTMANN CONCLUDES HIS FAMOUS 1941 lecture on de-mythologizing with the italicized words: "*Das Wort ward Fleisch*," or "*the word became flesh*."[1] The reference to John 1:14 is not merely a clever way to illustrate his thesis about the paradoxical identity of transcendence and immanence, of eternity and history. Nor is it merely indicative of the deeply Johannine character of Bultmann's theology. The reference to this verse instead points to something often overlooked, namely, the fact that Bultmann is perhaps best understood as a theologian of the incarnation, or better yet: a theologian of *Advent*.[2]

---

1. Bultmann, *Neues Testament*, 64. Cf. Bultmann, "New Testament," 42. I use the lowercase "word" because the use of "Word" is often associated with a metaphysical account of Christ that separates the *Word* from the human, historical *word* (i.e., the kerygma) in which we encounter him today. Bultmann, of course, has no such separation. Jesus Christ *is* the kerygmatic word of the gospel. For this reason I translate the German *Wort* consistently as "word" as a way of signaling Bultmann's approach to questions of christology.

2. In what follows I use "Advent" to refer to the liturgical season that celebrates the coming of Christ, and I use "advent" to refer to the actual event of Christ's eschatological coming.

THE THEOLOGY OF ADVENT

The importance of Advent to Bultmann's theology makes sense when we begin to see how this theme brings together the various elements that we have already explored. The starting place, of course, is eschatology. The celebration of Advent looks ahead to Christ's coming. It is a thoroughly eschatological season in the church year. The fact that the church celebrates the triumphant return of Christ at the same time as it celebrates Christ's humble birth—exemplified in the singing of hymns like "Joy to the World"—serves to make a subtle theological point that is at the heart of Bultmann's project, namely, that the coming of Jesus *is* the final eschatological event. As the Gospel of John says: "Now is the judgment of this world; now the ruler of this world will be driven out" (John 12:31). John captures this most profoundly with the use of light imagery. In the opening prologue, we read that "the light shines in the darkness, and the darkness did not overcome it" (John 1:5). Then later we read that "this is the judgment, that the light has come into the world" (John 3:19). Regarding this latter passage Bultmann writes in his commentary on John:

> There can be no mistaking the attack which this statement makes on traditional eschatology, even though the Evangelist does not specifically refer to it. Judgment for him is nothing more nor less than the fact that the "light," the Revealer, has come to the world. This saving event is judgment, for the reason that people . . . have shut themselves off from the "light."[3]

Bultmann puts it even more succinctly a little later: "the mission of Jesus is the eschatological event."[4] Paradoxi-

3. Bultmann, *Gospel*, 157.
4. Ibid., 159.

cally, the community of faith looks ahead to an event that has already happened. Or, from another perspective, they remember an event that is no mere datum of history but is the end of history itself. The future is already past, and the past is already future—which means that both past and future encounter us now in the present.

While church teaching separates incarnation and eschatological advent, church practice places them together in a way that is theologically suggestive. We might describe the simultaneity of Christmas and Advent using Bultmann's term "paradoxical identity." To illustrate what Bultmann means by this term, it helps to think of the shift from two-dimensional to three-dimensional vision. If we look at the world through just one eye, we accurately see what is around us, but everything appears flat. We see the objects on the surface, so to speak, but we do not comprehend their *depth*. Opening our other eye affords us a new perspective by which to observe the world. Our brains reconcile these two sets of images so that we perceive the world in a three-dimensional way. We see the *same object* in *two ways*. The two perspectives are nonidentical but coterminous. This description roughly approximates what Bultmann means by paradoxical identity: faith sees the two-dimensional historical occurrence in its three-dimensional theological significance. Applied to the above situation we can say: faith sees the birth of Jesus as the advent of the eschatological Lord, who comes to judge the living and the dead.

The paradoxical identity of incarnation and advent has certain implications. First, as already indicated, it is visible to faith alone, which means it is nonobjectifiable. If Christ's advent is not an occurrence on the plane of world history accessible in principle to any observer, then it is an event of history in the sense of *Geschichte*, the understanding of which simultaneously involves a new self-understanding.

We encounter the advent, therefore, in the same way that we encounter the incarnation, namely, in the form of kerygma, as proclamation and summons. To encounter the message of Christ's advent is to encounter a demand placed upon us by God. It is only fitting that the proclamation of Christ's coming to judge the living and the dead should itself be the occasion of a judgment upon me as the hearer of this word. This is to be expected, of course. For if Jesus is truly the Christ, then "Jesus is really present in the kerygma, [and] it is *his* word which involves the hearer in the kerygma."[5]

THE PROCLAMATION OF ADVENT

It is hardly surprising that the advent-character of Bultmann's theology is most plainly on display in his sermons. Bultmann regularly preached at the University of Marburg chapel, and some of his sermons have been published in two volumes, *Marburger Predigten* (translated as *This World and the Beyond*) and *Das verkündigte Wort* (*The Proclaimed Word*). Thirteen of the homilies in these volumes, delivered between 1907 and 1943, were preached during the liturgical seasons of Advent or Christmas. While we cannot explore each of these sermons in detail, an overview of the key passages and ideas will illuminate the importance of advent to Bultmann's theology.

Prior to becoming a dialectical theologian around 1920, Bultmann's Christmas-related sermons are noticeably different in tone and content. They are distinctively liberal in the tradition of Schleiermacher and Ritschl. He concludes a sermon titled "Love," delivered on December 26, 1910, by speaking about a "beautiful custom" on Christmas Eve in a region of Germany. When it becomes dark people leave their homes and come to the church where they light

5. Bultmann, "Primitive Christian Kerygma," 42.

candles, each person lighting the candle of the next person. Finally "the whole church is filled by the splendor of all the lights, each one receiving light from others and giving light to others. This is the image of a proper Christmas celebration."[6] Absent is any sense of encounter with Christ that demands a decision. The focus is on the religious piety and communal love that Christmas inspires.

The following year, on December 10, Bultmann preached on, "What does faith in the future mean for us?" The text for the sermon was 1 Corinthians 7:29–31, arguably the most important passage in his entire body of work, and certainly the text most associated with his theology. We see many of the dominant themes of his later work in this sermon. He begins by describing how "early Christianity was a religion of hope" that expected the coming of Jesus as the "heavenly king" who would establish his reign on earth.[7] The trouble is that "we all know we live in a great community of culture and work, and every day we enjoy its goods. . . . If we live for the future, it is a future in this world. If we believe in a future, it is the future our work creates."[8] He goes on to say that out of this common culture and work arises a "feeling [or sense] of community" (*Gemeinschaftsgefühl*) as well as the "great cultural goods of state and family."[9] We are clearly reading a prewar text. What Bultmann explores in the rest of the sermon is how to understand the relation between these cultural goods and the eternal future. He claims that faith "is not supported by our work but rather supports our work, helping us through weary hours, through despondency and despair."[10] The

6. Bultmann, *Das verkündigte Wort*, 55.

7. Ibid., 65.

8. Ibid., 66–67.

9. Ibid., 67.

10. Ibid., 72.

faith in the future that Advent brings to mind teaches us that, "as much as we are committed to work, what the outcome will be is *wholly* God's gift."[11] Despite being an Advent sermon, there is no talk about the coming of Christ. The sermon is entirely focused on the classic liberal themes of experience, feeling, culture, and community. Even talk of the future is abstract and this-worldly; it is the future of general human experience, not of God's eschatological action that demands obedience.

The contrast between these early Advent sermons and those following his dialectical turn in the early 1920s is stark. In place of beautiful customs and a generic faith in the future, there is instead the proclamation that an *event* has taken place that has fundamentally changed the world. He opens his sermon on December 19, 1924, by declaring that "we are not celebrating an idea but an event."[12] The theme of this text is not love in general but the Johannine claim that "*God* is love," which means that, where this love is concerned, "what takes place there is not something that can be understood as the result of a development, not even a moral development, but rather there takes place something new, something wondrous, which is in a true sense an event."[13] What is the nature of this event? Bultmann goes on to specify what he means:

> The statement "God is love" does not express an idea, a notion of the imagination, but rather it has a wholly concrete content: God forgives sin. That God forgives sin means God leads us from the sphere of the finite into the eternal, from the sphere of the Something into that of the Whole. God makes us new; God leads us from the old,

11. Ibid., 74.
12. Ibid., 208.
13. Ibid., 210–11.

> from the shadow, from death into the new, the
> light, the life—from appearance into reality.[14]

The key themes of dialectical theology appear in this passage: the emphasis on concrete reality (i.e., historicity) over against abstract ideas, the eschatological discontinuity between the old and new (what he calls "the great Either-Or"),[15] and most importantly of all, the centrality of divine action—specifically God's *saving* action.[16] Advent is no longer about supporting a "feeling of community" but about the eschatological arrival of salvation that judges our old existence and establishes a new one.

Later Advent and Christmas sermons further develop this position. If the advent of God is the eschatological turning-point of the ages, then we are confronted by the decision whether we will belong to the new age or cling to the old. A sermon on December 17, 1926, where he asks about the meaning of Christmas, makes this point in a way paradigmatic of the later Bultmann:

> The message of Christmas is: there is a *second beginning*; that event, "the word became flesh," is this beginning, in which love became a reality. How can love be a possibility for us, become a reality for us, if we come from hate? One way only: by the fact that we are loved. How can we become new, start a new beginning, get away from ourselves? One way only: through love

14. Ibid., 211–12.

15. Ibid., 214.

16. In the block quote, notice that "God" is the subject of a verb: "God forgives," "God leads," "God makes." This is no accident. Earlier that same year Bultmann had given a lecture on the new dialectical theologians in which he states: "The subject of theology is *God*, and the chief charge to be brought against liberal theology is that it has dealt not with God but with humanity" (Bultmann, "Liberal Theology," 29, rev.).

> that forgives. . . . Once again, we are confronted
> by the *choice* whether this beginning will be our
> beginning. It is not an event that has created ob-
> jective world-historical values that are bestowed
> on us without our choosing, which means
> without faith. It is not an event that has led to a
> world-historical occurrence, in whose so-called
> blessings we all readily participate. But instead
> it is an event that, as a beginning, is *always* a
> beginning. . . . When we say "always beginning"
> we thus mean: this event always demands our
> decision. We have to choose whether it will be a
> beginning for us.[17]

The talk of choice and decision—a prominent feature of Bultmann's theology—thus arises in conjunction with a greater appreciation of the *reality* of God's action. We might even speak of the "objectivity" of God's advent, so long as we distinguish this from the objectifiability of world history. Immediately following the above passage, Bultmann guards against the error of thinking that our decision determines whether the advent of Christ is a new beginning or not, which would seem to make the saving significance of his coming subject to our affirmation. On the contrary, the advent of Christ "*is* in fact always the beginning for us, whether we want it to be or not. We *choose* always only in which sense it will be the beginning for us. For ever since this event took place, all history has been marked by it."[18]

Statements like these are not typically associated with Bultmann as represented in standard theology textbooks. The image of Bultmann generally taught in North America is a theologian of sanitized, individualistic piety deprived of his robust faith in God's radically new and invasive action

17. Bultmann, *Das verkündigte Wort*, 236–37.
18. Ibid., 238.

in Christ. We cannot understand his talk of decision if we fail to see that this is the personal response demanded by the *reality* of what God has done. Faith-as-decision is the subjective correlate of God's objective action.

In his sermon on December 16, 1931, Bultmann seeks to clarify his position on this matter. He asks what it means to anticipate one who has already come. Does Advent make sense, given that Christmas is already in the past? To address this question, he begins by elucidating the nature of Christ's advent: "The coming of the Lord, which the Christian community anticipates in Advent and celebrates at Christmas, is not at all primarily his coming to the individual, his entering into the soul, but rather his coming to the *world*." He then cites one of his favorite lines from Luther—"the eternal light enters in, giving the *world* a new appearance"—which appears in five sermons in *Das verkündigte Wort* and once in *Marburger Predigten*.[19] As in the 1926 sermon, Bultmann is at pains to make sure people understand that the Christ-event is not a mere possibility that only becomes an actuality in our response to it. On the contrary, "God's word is . . . that the Lord *has* come, that the eternal light *has* given the world a new appearance." For this reason, "if we are serious in the expectation of the coming one, then *we await one who has already come, who is already here*."[20]

Bultmann is here touching on one of the central paradoxes in Christianity. On the one hand, our confessions, liturgies, and religious experiences attest to the deeply held conviction that Christ is with us today, just as truly as he was with his disciples. The Gospel of Matthew indicates this in its famous closing line, which has Jesus telling his followers: "And remember, I am with you always, to the end of the age"

19. Ibid., 240.
20. Ibid.

(Matt 28:20). On the other hand, of course, Jesus is no longer physically present. If presence is construed in strictly physical terms, then Christians expect the coming of one who is actually *absent*, for whom the Holy Spirit serves as a surrogate in the time between the times. Bultmann, however, follows the Johannine understanding of Christ as the eternal word of God (John 1:1, 14), and of faith as our abiding in Christ (John 6:56; 15:4–10; 1 John 2:24; 3:24). In other words, there is a significant strand of NT tradition that already differentiates between Christ's presence and his physical proximity, so that the former can exist without the latter.

When Bultmann thus asks, "*how* is he here?" he responds emphatically: "In his *word!*"[21] As a word-event, the fact that Christ *has come* does not preclude or conflict with his coming *again* ever anew. On the contrary, it is because he is "already here" in the word that we can confidently expect to encounter him yet again. But "*how* is this word the light that gives the world a new appearance?"[22] Bultmann answers this in his own characteristic way by referring to John 3:19: "And this is the judgment, that the light has come into the world, and people loved darkness rather than light because their deeds were evil." The coming of the eternal word and light of God places before us the decisive question "whether we love the light or the darkness."[23] The event of God's advent thus occurs "in the moment of decision."[24] We must decide whether we will cling to the old world or participate in the new world inbreaking in Christ, for the light that has entered the world in Jesus "does not illuminate the world the way we would like to see it, . . . but rather

21. Ibid.
22. Ibid., 241.
23. Ibid., 243.
24. Ibid., 246.

it gives the world a *new* appearance."[25] The world is in fact truly new because of Christ's advent, though it only takes on its transfigured appearance for the eyes of faith. The one who hears and responds obediently to the word sees the world in a new way.

His sermon on December 11, 1938, connects the new appearance of the world with the eschatological freedom of faith. In this address Bultmann comments on Jesus' response to John the Baptist's question, "Are you the one who is to come?" (Matt 11:3), in which Jesus describes the things he has done, such as giving the blind sight, giving the deaf hearing, and preaching good news to the poor. As Bultmann puts it, "where Christ holds sway, miraculous things happen. . . . And where does Christ hold sway? Wherever the word of the gospel is preached and heard."[26] And what is the gospel?

> In a word: freedom from this world. The gospel has the power to grant freedom from the world, because it is the message of God's grace and the forgiveness of sins. This word makes the world new for those who believe. He who is to come has in truth come and has renewed the world— renewed for those who allow themselves to be renewed by him. . . . Through his coming our outlook on the world and on time is completely changed. His coming is not an event within the process of world history, which immediately becomes part of the past; rather it is an event that signifies the end of world history.[27]

25. Ibid., 242.

26. Bultmann, *This World*, 107–8, rev. A genuine miracle in this sense is "simply every manifestation of Christian love that strikes us, shames us, shocks and quickens us" (ibid., 108, rev.).

27. Ibid., 109–10, rev.

Christ's coming *to* the world coincides with faith's freedom *from* the world in the sense that Christ brings an end to the old age, thus freeing the believer from sin and death. As Bultmann points out in a sermon on December 14, 1939, such freedom is "not simply a feeling of alienation from the world, not simply something negative. Rather it is just the consciousness of living in the fullness of the power of an otherworldly, genuine reality."[28] A true miracle thus occurs when we live out of this transcendent power. When that occurs, the world is renewed for the person of faith, and it is this renewal of all things to which the Gospel accounts bear witness in the stories of the blind seeing and the lame walking.

THE PRACTICE OF PERPETUAL ADVENT

Bultmann concludes his sermon on December 12, 1943, with the following words:

> To be a Christian means to be one who waits for God's future. *Hence for the Christian perhaps all seasons are essentially an Advent season.* For Advent is characterized above all by this note of expectation. . . . It is intended to remind us sharply of what we so easily and so often forget, namely that, as Christians, we are expectant.[29]

In the same way that every season is essentially a time of Advent, so too every dimension of Bultmann's theology is essentially an advent-theology, something which this brief introduction to his theology has hopefully illustrated. Advent is rarely as overt in his theological writings as it is in his sermons, but it is no less present, even if only operating at the level of the underlying theological grammar or

28. Ibid., 117, rev.
29. Ibid., 210. Emphasis mine.

conceptual framework. Expectation and promise are infused throughout Bultmann's writings. It is the expectation not of the literal return of Christ, nor of a miracle of nature, but of the hearing of God's word and promise to us in the gospel. As the arrival of God's word, the advent is not a single occurrence in the past, like other events of world history. It is rather an event that always *remains* an event, and so always demands a fresh decision of faith. We may accurately speak of Bultmann as a *theologian of perpetual advent*, not because, like Origen, the Logos is present in creation apart from the person of Jesus,[30] but because Christ himself is the word-event that perpetually occurs anew wherever the emancipatory, eschatological freedom from the world that defines the kerygma takes hold of a person.

The Christian must therefore adopt a posture and practice of perpetual expectancy. Every moment is an opportunity to encounter Christ and open oneself to "the gift of God's future."[31] For those who participate by faith in God's renewal of all things, every day holds the possibility of becoming the occasion of Christ's advent. This, above all, is the lesson to learn from reading and reflecting on Bultmann's rich body of work.

QUESTIONS FOR REFLECTION

1. Does the coming of Christ bring about a new *possibility* or a new *actuality*?

2. What does it mean to say that the "*word* became flesh"? Has talk of the "Word" become too familiar to us in the church? How might it change our thinking about christology if we say that the "*kerygma* became flesh" or the "*eschaton* became flesh"?

30. See Tzamalikos, *Origen*, 66.
31. Bultmann, *This World*, 210.

3. Bultmann says that the gospel is "freedom from this world" because the advent of God's word "makes the world new for those who believe." How does this conception relate to ancient ascetic theology or to contemporary apocalyptic theology? How is it similar to and different from gnosticism?

4. How might a person *practice* the belief in perpetual advent? What might such expectancy look like in a world of mass anxiety about terrorism, climate change, and economic collapse?

FURTHER READING

IF THIS BRIEF INTRODUCTION to Bultmann's theology has stimulated your interest, I recommend the following books (arranged chronologically) to delve further into his life and work.

Karl Barth and Rudolf Bultmann, *Karl Barth – Rudolf Bultmann Letters, 1922–1966*, trans. Geoffrey W. Bromiley (Grand Rapids: Eerdmans, 1981).

The revealing letters between Barth and Bultmann touch on many of the key events and debates in twentieth-century theology and provide crucial insight into Bultmann's understanding of hermeneutics, philosophy, and the kerygma, among other topics.

Rudolf Bultmann, *New Testament and Mythology and Other Basic Writings*, ed. Schubert Ogden (Minneapolis: Fortress, 1984).

Superbly translated by Ogden, this collection of essays provides the best introduction to Bultmann's later theology and hermeneutics, including his program of demythologizing. The essay, "Theology as Science," was published posthumously in German in the same year and is essential reading. The 1952 essay, "On the Program of Demythologizing," clarifies many of the questions raised by the programmatic 1941 essay that opens the volume.

James F. Kay, *Christus Praesens: A Reconsideration of Rudolf Bultmann's Christology* (Grand Rapids: Eerdmans, 1994).

This excellent study of Bultmann's christology clears up much of the confusion regarding Bultmann's understanding of the historical Jesus and the kerygmatic Christ, in relation to both his teachers and his later critics.

Rudolf Bultmann, *What Is Theology?*, trans. Roy A. Harrisville (Minneapolis: Fortress, 1997).

When *Theologische Enzyklopädie* was first published in 1984—compiled by Eberhard Jüngel and Klaus W. Müller from Bultmann's lectures in theology between 1926 and 1936—it revealed that Bultmann was a systematic theologian in his own right. The historical context is important, and readers need to pay attention to the letters in the text that indicate from which set of lectures a passage derives. On many of the themes addressed in this introduction, *What Is Theology?* is an indispensable resource.

Christophe Chalamet, *Dialectical Theologians: Wilhelm Herrmann, Karl Barth and Rudolf Bultmann* (Zürich: TVZ, 2005).

For those more academically inclined, Christophe Chalamet's study of Herrmann, Barth, and Bultmann is a feast of intellectual delights. Chalamet argues that Bultmann, like Barth, is a consistently dialectical theologian who learned to think dialectically from his Marburg professor, Wilhelm Herrmann.

Konrad Hammann, *Rudolf Bultmann: A Biography*, trans. Philip E. Devenish (Salem, OR: Polebridge, 2013).

Hammann's magisterial biography of Bultmann is a rich historical and theological resource. Hammann not only situates Bultmann within his historical context, but he also provides insightful interpretations of his writings, many of which need to be located historically in order to be fully understood. A must-have book for anyone interested in Bultmann.

BIBLIOGRAPHY

Barth, Karl. *Church Dogmatics*. Edited by G. W. Bromiley and T. F. Torrance. 4 vols. Edinburgh: T. & T. Clark, 1956–1975.

———. *The Epistle to the Romans*. Translated by Edwyn C. Hoskyns. London: Oxford University Press, 1933. Reprint, 1968.

———. *Evangelical Theology: An Introduction*. New York: Holt, 1963.

———. *Offene Briefe* 1909–1935. Edited by Diether Koch. Gesamtausgabe 5. Zürich: TVZ, 2001.

———. *Der Römerbrief (Zweite Fassung)* 1922. Edited by Cornelis van der Kooi and Katja Tolstaja. Gesamtausgabe 2. Zürich: TVZ, 2010.

Bousset, Wilhelm. *Kyrios Christos: Geschichte des Christusglaubens von den Anfängen des Christentums bis Irenaeus*. Göttingen: Vandenhoeck & Ruprecht, 1913.

Bultmann, Rudolf. "Adam and Christ according to Romans 5." In *Current Issues in New Testament Interpretation: Essays in Honor of Otto A. Piper*, edited by William Klassen and Graydon F. Snyder, 143–65. New York: Harper & Brothers, 1962.

———. "Der Arier-Paragraph im Raume der Kirche." *Theologische Blätter* 12 (1933) 359–70.

———. "Autobiographical Reflections." In *The Theology of Rudolf Bultmann*, edited by Charles W. Kegley, xix–xxv. New York: Harper & Row, 1966.

———. "The Christological Confession of the World Council of Churches [1951–52]." In *Essays, Philosophical and Theological*, 273–90. New York: Macmillan, 1955.

———. "The Christology of the New Testament [1933]." In *Faith and Understanding*, edited by Robert W. Funk, 262–85. Philadelphia: Fortress, 1987.

———. "Church and Teaching in the New Testament [1929]." In *Faith and Understanding*, edited by Robert W. Funk, 184–219. Philadelphia: Fortress, 1987.

———. "The Concept of the Word of God in the New Testament [1933]." In *Faith and Understanding*, edited by Robert W. Funk, 286–312. Philadelphia: Fortress, 1987.

———. "The Eschatology of the Gospel of John [1928]." In *Faith and Understanding*, edited by Robert W. Funk, 165–83. Philadelphia: Fortress, 1987.

———. "Ethical and Mystical Religion in Primitive Christianity." In *The Beginnings of Dialectic Theology*, edited by James M. Robinson, 221–35. Richmond: John Knox, 1968.

———. "Der Gedanke der Freiheit nach antikem und christlichem Verständnis [1959]." In *Glauben und Verstehen: Gesammelte Aufsätze*, 4 vols., 4:42–51. Tübingen: Mohr, 1933–1965.

———. *Geschichte und Eschatologie*. Tübingen: Mohr, 1958.

———. *Glauben und Verstehen: Gesammelte Aufsätze*. 4 vols. Tübingen: J. C. B. Mohr, 1933–1965.

———. *The Gospel of John: A Commentary*. Translated by G. R. Beasley-Murray et al. Philadelphia: Westminster, 1971.

———. *History and Eschatology: The Gifford Lectures* 1955. Edinburgh: Edinburgh University Press, 1957.

———. "Humanism and Christianity." *Journal of Religion* 32, no. 2 (1952) 77–86.

———. "Humanism and Christianity [1948]." In *Essays, Philosophical and Theological*, 151–67. New York: Macmillan, 1955.

———. "In eigener Sache [1957]." In *Glauben und Verstehen: Gesammelte Aufsätze*, 4 vols., 3:178–89. Tübingen: Mohr, 1933–1965.

———. "Is Exegesis Without Presuppositions Possible? [1957]." In *New Testament and Mythology and Other Basic Writings*, edited by Schubert M. Ogden, 145–53. Philadelphia: Fortress, 1984.

———. "Ist die Apokalyptik die Mutter der christlichen Theologie? Eine Auseinandersetzung mit Ernst Käsemann [1964]." In *Exegetica: Aufsätze zur Erforschung des Neuen Testaments*, edited by Erich Dinkler, 476–82. Tübingen: Mohr, 1967.

———. *Jesus Christ and Mythology*. New York: Scribner, 1958.

———. "Liberal Theology and the Latest Theological Movement [1924]." In *Faith and Understanding*, edited by Robert W. Funk, 28–52. Philadelphia: Fortress, 1987.

———. *Marburger Predigten*. Tübingen: J. C. B. Mohr, 1956.

———. "Milestones in Books. IV." *Expository Times* 70, no. 4 (1959) 125.

————. *Neues Testament und Mythologie: Das Problem der Entmythologisierung der neutestamentlichen Verkündigung.* Edited by Eberhard Jüngel. Munich: Chr. Kaiser Verlag, 1985.

————. "New Testament and Mythology: The Problem of Demythologizing the New Testament Proclamation [1941]." In *New Testament and Mythology and Other Basic Writings*, edited by Schubert M. Ogden, 1–43. Philadelphia: Fortress, 1984.

————. "On Behalf of Christian Freedom." *Journal of Religion* 40, no. 2 (1960) 95–99.

————. "On the Concept of 'Myth' (1942–1952)." In David W. Congdon, *The Mission of Demythologizing: Rudolf Bultmann's Dialectical Theology*, 853–63. Minneapolis: Fortress, 2015.

————. "On the Problem of Demythologizing (1952)." In *New Testament and Mythology and Other Basic Writings*, edited by Schubert M. Ogden, 95–130. Philadelphia: Fortress, 1984.

————. "On the Question of Christology [1927]." In *Faith and Understanding*, edited by Robert W. Funk, 116–44. Philadelphia: Fortress, 1987.

————. "The Primitive Christian Kerygma and the Historical Jesus." In *The Historical Jesus and the Kerygmatic Christ: Essays on the New Quest of the Historical Jesus*, edited by Carl E. Braaten and Roy A. Harrisville, 15–42. New York: Abingdon, 1964.

————. "The Problem of 'Natural Theology' [1933]." In *Faith and Understanding*, edited by Robert W. Funk, 313–31. Philadelphia: Fortress, 1987.

————. "The Problem of a Theological Exegesis of the New Testament." In *The Beginnings of Dialectic Theology*, edited by James M. Robinson, 236–56. Richmond: John Knox, 1968.

————. "The Problem of Hermeneutics [1950]." In *New Testament and Mythology and Other Basic Writings*, edited by Schubert M. Ogden, 69–93. Philadelphia: Fortress, 1984.

————. "Protestant Theology and Atheism." *Journal of Religion* 52, no. 4 (1972) 331–35.

————. "Science and Existence [1955]." In *New Testament and Mythology and Other Basic Writings*, edited by Schubert M. Ogden, 131–44. Philadelphia: Fortress, 1984.

————. "The Significance of 'Dialectical Theology' for the Scientific Study of the New Testament [1928]." In *Faith and Understanding*, edited by Robert W. Funk, 145–64. Philadelphia: Fortress, 1987.

————. "The Significance of the Idea of Freedom for Western Civilization [1952]." In *Essays, Philosophical and Theological*, 305–25. New York: Macmillan, 1955.

————. *Theologie als Kritik: Ausgewählte Rezensionen und Forschungsberichte*. Edited by Matthias Dreher and Klaus W. Müller. Tübingen: Mohr Siebeck, 2002.

————. "Theology as Science [1941]." In *New Testament and Mythology and Other Basic Writings*, edited by Schubert M. Ogden, 45–67. Philadelphia: Fortress, 1984.

————. *Theology of the New Testament*. Translated by Kendrick Grobel. 2 vols. New York: Scribner, 1951–1955.

————. *This World and the Beyond: Marburg Sermons*. New York: Scribner, 1960.

————. *Das verkündigte Wort: Predigten, Andachten, Ansprachen* 1906–1941. Edited by Erich Grässer and Martin Evang. Tübingen: Mohr, 1984.

————. *Wachen und Träumen: Märchen*. Edited by Werner Zager. Berlin: Wichern, 2011.

————. "What Does It Mean to Speak of God? [1925]." In *Faith and Understanding*, edited by Robert W. Funk, 53–65. Philadelphia: Fortress, 1987.

————. *What Is Theology?* Translated by Roy A. Harrisville. Minneapolis: Fortress, 1997.

Bultmann, Rudolf, and Günther Bornkamm. *Briefwechsel* 1926–1976. Edited by Werner Zager. Tübingen: Mohr Siebeck, 2014.

Bultmann, Rudolf, and Martin Heidegger. *Briefwechsel* 1925–1975. Edited by Andreas Grossmann and Christof Landmesser. Tübingen: Mohr Siebeck, 2009.

Buri, Fritz. "Entmythologisierung oder Entkerygmatisierung der Theologie." In *Kerygma und Mythos, Band II: Diskussion und Stimmen zum Problem der Entmythologisierung*, edited by Hans-Werner Bartsch, 85–101. Hamburg-Volksdorf: Herbert Reich, 1952.

Busch, Eberhard. "God Is God: The Meaning of a Controversial Formula and the Fundamental Problem of Speaking about God." *Princeton Seminary Bulletin* 7, no. 2 (1986) 101–13.

Buschart, W. David, and Kent Eilers. *Theology as Retrieval: Receiving the Past, Renewing the Church*. Downers Grove: IVP Academic, 2015.

Calvin, John. *Institutes of the Christian Religion*. Edited by John T. McNeill. Translated by Ford Lewis Battles. 2 vols. Library of Christian Classics. Louisville: Westminster John Knox, 2006.

Chalamet, Christophe. *Dialectical Theologians: Wilhelm Herrmann, Karl Barth and Rudolf Bultmann*. Zürich: TVZ, 2005.

Bibliography

Cohen, Hermann. *Logik der reinen Erkenntniss.* System der Philosophie 1. Berlin: Cassirer, 1902.

Congdon, David W. *The Mission of Demythologizing: Rudolf Bultmann's Dialectical Theology.* Minneapolis: Fortress, 2015.

———. "The Trinitarian Shape of πίστις: A Theological Exegesis of Galatians." *Journal of Theological Interpretation* 2, no. 2 (2008) 231–58.

Ebeling, Gerhard. "Kerygma [1964]." In *Wort und Glaube, Dritter Band: Beiträge zur Fundamentaltheologie, Soteriologie und Ekklesiologie,* 515–21. Tübingen: J. C. B. Mohr, 1975.

———. "The Significance of the Critical Historical Method for Church and Theology in Protestantism [1950]." In *Word and Faith,* 17–61. Philadelphia: Fortress, 1963.

———. *Theology and Proclamation: Dialogue with Bultmann.* Translated by John Riches. Philadelphia: Fortress, 1966.

———. "Word of God and Hermeneutics [1959]." In *Word and Faith,* 305–32. Philadelphia: Fortress, 1963.

"An Existential Way of Reading the Bible." *Time,* May 22, 1964, 86.

Funk, Robert W. Introduction to *Faith and Understanding,* 9–27. Philadelphia: Fortress, 1987.

Grässer, Erich. "Albert Schweitzer und Rudolf Bultmann: Ein Beitrag zur historischen Jesusfrage." In *Rudolf Bultmanns Werk und Wirkung,* edited by Bernd Jaspert, 53–69. Darmstadt: Wissenschaftliche Buchgesellschaft, 1984.

Hammann, Konrad. *Rudolf Bultmann: A Biography.* Translated by Philip E. Devenish. Salem, OR: Polebridge, 2013.

Harvey, Van A. *The Historian and the Believer: The Morality of Historical Knowledge and Christian Belief.* New York: Macmillan, 1966.

Hector, Kevin W. *Theology without Metaphysics: God, Language, and the Spirit of Recognition.* Cambridge: Cambridge University Press, 2011.

Heidegger, Martin. *Being and Time.* Rev. ed. of the Stambaugh Translation. Edited by Dennis J. Schmidt. Translated by Joan Stambaugh. Albany: SUNY Press, 2010.

Herrmann, Wilhelm. *The Communion of the Christian with God: A Discussion in Agreement with the View of Luther.* Translated by J. Sandys Stanyon. London: Williams & Norgate, 1895.

Jüngel, Eberhard. "Glauben und Verstehen: Zum Theologiebegriff Rudolf Bultmanns." In *Wertlose Wahrheit: Zur Identität und Relevanz des christlichen Glaubens – Theologische Erörterungen III,* 16–77. Munich: Chr. Kaiser, 1990.

————. *God's Being Is in Becoming: The Trinitarian Being of God in the Theology of Karl Barth; A Paraphrase.* Translated by John Webster. Grand Rapids: Eerdmans, 2001.

————. *Justification: The Heart of the Christian Faith.* Translated by Jeffrey F. Cayzer. Edinburgh: T. & T. Clark, 2001.

Kähler, Martin. *The So-Called Historical Jesus and the Historic Biblical Christ.* Translated by Carl E. Braaten. Philadelphia: Fortress, 1964.

Käsemann, Ernst. *New Testament Questions of Today.* Translated by W. J. Montague. London: SCM Press, 1969.

Kay, James F. *Christus Praesens: A Reconsideration of Rudolf Bultmann's Christology.* Grand Rapids: Eerdmans, 1994.

Kelly, Geffrey B. "'Unconscious Christianity' and the 'Anonymous Christian' in the Theology of Dietrich Bonhoeffer and Karl Rahner." *Philosophy & Theology* 9, no. 1–2 (1995) 117–49.

Koch, Klaus. *The Rediscovery of Apocalyptic: A Polemical Work on a Neglected Area of Biblical Studies and Its Damaging Effects on Theology and Philosophy.* Translated by Margaret Kohl. London: SCM Press, 1972.

Kolb, Robert, and Timothy J. Wengert, eds. *The Book of Concord: The Confessions of the Evangelical Lutheran Church.* Minneapolis: Fortress, 2000.

Lacan, Jacques. *The Ego in Freud's Theory and in the Technique of Psychoanalysis, 1954–1955.* The Seminar of Jacques Lacan Book 2. New York: Norton, 1988.

Lamoureux, Denis O. "Evangelicals Inheriting the Wind: The Phillip E. Johnson Phenomenon." In *Darwinism Defeated? The Johnson-Lamoureux Debate on Biological Origins,* 9–48. Vancouver: Regent College Publishing, 1999.

————. *Evolutionary Creation: A Christian Approach to Evolution.* Eugene, OR: Wipf & Stock, 2008.

Lewis, C. S. *An Experiment in Criticism.* Cambridge: Cambridge University Press, 1961.

Luther, Martin. "The Large Catechism." In *The Book of Concord: The Confessions of the Evangelical Lutheran Church,* edited by Robert Kolb and Timothy J. Wengert, 377–480. Minneapolis: Fortress, 2000.

————. *Luther's Works.* Edited by Jaroslav Pelikan and Helmut T. Lehman. American ed. 55 vols. Philadelphia: Fortress, 1955–72.

Martyn, J. Louis. "Epistemology at the Turn of the Ages." In *Theological Issues in the Letters of Paul,* 89–110. Nashville: Abingdon, 1997.

McCormack, Bruce L. *Karl Barth's Critically Realistic Dialectical Theology: Its Genesis and Development,* 1909–1936. New York: Oxford University Press, 1995.

Meeks, Wayne A. "The Problem of Christian Living." In *Beyond Bultmann: Reckoning a New Testament Theology,* edited by Bruce W. Longenecker and Mikeal C. Parsons, 211–29. Waco, TX: Baylor University Press, 2014.

Migliore, Daniel L. "*Veni Creator Spiritus*: The Work of the Spirit in the Theologies of B. B. Warfield and Karl Barth." In *Karl Barth and the Making of Evangelical Theology: A Fifty-Year Perspective,* edited by Clifford B. Anderson and Bruce L. McCormack, 157–77. Grand Rapids: Eerdmans, 2015.

Natorp, Paul. *Allgemeine Psychologie nach kritischer Methode.* Tübingen: Mohr, 1912.

Ogden, Schubert M. *Christ without Myth: A Study Based on the Theology of Rudolf Bultmann.* New York: Harper, 1961.

Pine, Lisa. *Education in Nazi Germany.* Oxford: Berg, 2010.

Ross, Hugh. *The Creator and the Cosmos: How the Greatest Scientific Discoveries of the Century Reveal God.* Colorado Springs: NavPress, 1993.

Rowe, C. Kavin. "The Kerygma of the Earliest Church." In *Beyond Bultmann: Reckoning a New Testament Theology,* edited by Bruce W. Longenecker and Mikeal C. Parsons, 23–37. Waco, TX: Baylor University Press, 2014.

Schleiermacher, Friedrich. *Hermeneutics and Criticism and Other Writings.* Edited by Andrew Bowie. Cambridge: Cambridge University Press, 1998.

Schmithals, Walter. *An Introduction to the Theology of Rudolf Bultmann.* Minneapolis: Augsburg, 1968.

———. "Nachwort." In Bultmann, *Jesus,* 149–58.

Schroeder, Henry J. *Canons and Decrees of the Council of Trent.* Rockford, IL: Tan, 1978.

Schweitzer, Albert. *The Quest of the Historical Jesus.* Translated by John Bowden. Minneapolis: Fortress, 2001.

Standhartinger, Angela. "Bultmann's *Theology of the New Testament* in Context." In *Beyond Bultmann: Reckoning a New Testament Theology,* edited by Bruce W. Longenecker and Mikeal C. Parsons, 233–55. Waco, TX: Baylor University Press, 2014.

Tillich, Paul. *Perspectives on 19th and 20th Century Protestant Theology.* Edited by Carl E. Braaten. New York: Harper & Row, 1967.

Tzamalikos, Panagiōtēs. *Origen: Philosophy of History and Eschatology.* Supplements to Vigiliae Christianae 85. Leiden: Brill, 2007.

Walton, John H. *The Lost World of Genesis One: Ancient Cosmology and the Origins Debate.* Downers Grove: IVP Academic, 2009.

Watson, Francis. "Hermeneutics and the Doctrine of Scripture: Why They Need Each Other." *International Journal of Systematic Theology* 12, no. 2 (2010) 118–43.

Weiss, Johannes. *Die Predigt Jesu vom Reiche Gottes.* Göttingen: Vandenhoeck & Ruprecht, 1892.

———. *Jesus' Proclamation of the Kingdom of God.* Philadelphia: Fortress, 1971.Subject Index

SUBJECT INDEX

address   70, 72–74
advent   10, 146–58
ancient Near East   121
anthropomorphism   108
apocalyptic   3, 7–10, 12,
                   14, 95, 97, 106
Aristotle   133
Asmussen, Hans   130
Augsburg Confession   41
Augustine of Hippo   81–82, 113
authenticity (*Eigentlichkeit*)
                             82, 122–23
authorial intention   125–26
autonomy   131–33, 140–41
Baier, Johann Wilhelm   41
Barth, Karl   7, 14, 16–18, 29–30,
               52–53, 56, 72, 84n54, 89,
                   92–93, 144n42
Bonhoeffer, Dietrich   83n51
Bornkamm, Günther   130
Bousset, Wilhelm   16
Braaten, Carl   89
Brunner, Emil   15
Buri, Fritz   76
Calvin, John   26n37
christology   29n40,
               49–50, 64–69, 72, 98,
                   106–7, 146n1
        See also Jesus

church
    early Christian community
                   3, 10, 14, 64–65, 106
    as empirical and eschatological
                   77–78, 91
    and kerygma   56–57,
                   64–66, 76–78
    proclamation of   72, 74–75
classical theism   26–27
Cohen, Hermann   43–44
compatibilism   27
concordism   124–27
Confessing Church   77, 108,
                             130n4
content criticism (*Sachkritik*) 75,
                   115, 117–19
content exegesis (*Sachexegese*)
                             117–18
contextualization   121
cosmology   125
Council of Trent   39
creationism   124n27
Dasein   45
decision   28, 55, 58, 74, 84n54,
               115, 122, 135–36, 150,
                   153–55, 158
dekerygmatizing   76
demythologizing
    (*Entmythologisierung*)
               5, 9, 42, 79, 101, 104–5,
                   107–10, 114, 119–20,
                   136n24, 137–38, 146
denazification   129–30
deus ex machina   110
deworldlizing (*Entweltlichung*)
                             136n24
dialectical theology. *See* theology,
                   dialectical
Easter   97–98
Ebeling, Gerhard   62–63,
                   69–70, 113–14

171

epistemology   1, 33, 36,
        42–43, 53–55
eschatological event   29, 49, 56,
        66, 69, 77, 96–99, 123,
        147, 151
eschatology   1–13, 14–15,
        29–30, 40, 78, 95–99,
        106, 115, 147, 152
    as break in history (*krisis*) 91,
        96–97, 156
    future   3, 7, 10, 104, 106
    inaugurated   10
    mythological   8–9
    realized   10
evangelicalism   124, 126
exegesis. *See* interpretation
existentialism   21–22, 30,
        121, 123
Existenz   44–45
faith   21, 22n23, 36–43, 50, 60,
        64–66, 68–69, 73, 81–82,
        87, 105, 136, 138–39
    by faith alone (*sola fide*)   36,
        41–43, 46, 114, 148, 156
    deed rather than work
        37–38, 41, 47, 75
    going out into utter darkness
        12, 134, 138, 139, 140,
        143
    and history   88–89,
        91–99
    in the church   76–77
    in the future   150–51
    in humanity   132–33
    as obedience   28, 37,
        57–58, 68, 74, 122
    unconscious/unreflective
        79–80, 82–84
    See also self-understanding
fascism   140

flesh (*sarx*)   33–36,
        47–48, 58, 98, 122
    "according to the flesh"   34–
        36, 47–49, 55, 60, 92–94,
        99, 110–11
freedom   96, 132–44, 156–57
    as eschatological event   136
    and law   137
    negative   140
    as obedience   134
free will   26–29
Frei, Hans   141
German Christians   77–78
Geschichte. See history, as
        Historie and *Geschichte*
gnosticism   34n5, 135
God
    action of   6, 46, 83, 152–54
    being of   49, 51, 115
    concept of   19, 21, 23–25
    as Creator   79
    freedom of   72, 78, 138, 143
    futurity of   115, 134, 144
    as given entity   48–49
    grace of   22, 24, 72,
        135–36, 143, 156
    hiddenness of   36n11
    judgment of   9
    knowledge of   21–22,
        26n37, 29, 42, 48–50, 57,
        60, 81–83, 110–11
    as love   151
    as nonobjectifiable   32–51,
        60, 72, 99, 108–9, 148
    omnipotence of   79, 110
    question about   81–82
    reality of   19–22, 25
    sovereignty of   26–29
    speaking of   17, 19–27,
        29, 50, 108–10

as wholly other 23–26, 32, 108–9, 115, 134

Gogarten, Friedrich 7, 14, 16–17

Greek philosophy 49, 55, 67, 134

Gross, Erwin 138–39

handiness (*Zuhandenheit*) 45n33

Harnack, Adolf von 92–93

Harvey, Van 86–87

Heidegger, Martin 44–49, 64, 71, 121–23, 123n25

Heilsgeschichte 91, 95

hermeneutics 80, 108, 112–27

Herrmann, Wilhelm 5–6, 50

Hirsch, Emanuel 93

historical consciousness 86–89, 113–14

historicity 29, 55, 84n54, 152

Historie. See history, as *Historie* and *Geschichte*

history 38, 86–99, 114, 153, 156, 158
   as empirical 91, 96–97
   and eschatology 99, 106
   as historical criticism 31, 92–93, 114
   as historical science 67, 86–90, 92–93
   as *Historie* and *Geschichte* 89–98, 148

Hollaz, David 41

Holy Spirit. *See* Spirit

humanism 130–35, 140

immanence and transcendence 7, 23, 32, 35, 41, 106, 109, 134, 146

imputation. *See* righteousness, imputed

individualism 22, 60–61n11, 140

inerrancy 113, 141

intercultural communication 107

interpretation 11, 72–73, 80, 87, 90–91, 101, 107–8, 112–16
   existentialist 53, 119–23
   subjective 59, 114
   theological 141–42
   without translation 125–27
   See also concordism; hermeneutics

Israel 34–35, 91–92, 95

Jesus (Christ)
   as criterion of the NT 118–19
   as crucified and risen 64–66, 68–70, 97–99
   eschatological coming of 147–49, 150, 153–54, 157
   historical 5, 16, 34, 49, 88, 92–99, 107, 116
   incarnation of 146, 148–49
   as Lord 71–73, 76
   paradox of 77, 98–99
   personality of 65, 68
   present in the word 50, 69–70, 98, 149, 155–56
   as proclaimer and proclaimed 28, 64–66
   as prophet 65–66, 94, 97
   as Revealer 98, 147
   See also christology; eschatological event

John (Johannine) 33, 98, 122, 146–47, 155

Judaism 65, 121

Second Temple 8n13, 95

justification 24, 36, 39–43, 58–60, 69, 71, 97, 114

Kähler, Martin 89

Käsemann, Ernst 3

Kant, Immanuel 3

Kay, James F.　62n1
Kelsey, David　141
kerygma　17, 56, 62–84, 97–98,
　　116–23, 127, 139, 149
　and church　56–57,
　　64–66, 76–78
　as church proclamation
　　about Jesus　64–67, 69
　criticism of Bultmann on　76
　and culture　78, 106–7
　distinction from theology
　　71–75, 77
　as encounter　75–77,
　　116–17, 119
　and myth　104
　as norm　77, 119n15,
　　123–24, 126–27
　as prelinguistic　74–75, 78, 83
　as word-event　68–73, 116,
　　120, 123, 158
　See also church, and kerygma
kingdom of God　2–7, 11
Kirchenkampf　77
Kümmel, Werner　10
Lacan, Jacques　25
Ladd, George Eldon　10
Lamoureux, Denis　126
law　37, 133–34, 137
legalism　139, 143
　liberalism. See theology, liberal
liberation　70, 83, 123
libertarianism　140
literalism　108–9
Luther, Martin (Lutheranism)
　　36–40, 50, 70, 118–19,
　　138–39, 154
Martyn, J. Louis　36n10
Meeks, Wayne　76
Melanchthon, Philipp　50, 120
metaphysics　24, 49
Migliore, Daniel　144n42

miracles　50–51, 83, 110,
　　156n26, 157–58
modernity　1, 3, 16, 107,
　　113, 140–43
molinism　27n38
myth/mythology　8, 42, 98,
　　101–11, 138
　as objectification　108–10,
　　118
　real intention of 42, 102, 109,
　　117, 119–20, 136n24
　and science　102–4,
　　109–10
　truth of　103–5, 109, 118
　See also world-picture
Nazi regime　60n11, 129–31, 134
Natorp, Paul　43
Neokantianism　43–44, 48–49
objectification (Objektivierung)
　　36, 42–44, 50, 60, 77–78,
　　93, 108–10, 144
objective presence
　　(Vorhandenheit)　37,
　　44–49, 54–55, 60, 121
Oden, Thomas　141
Ogden, Schubert　76
open theism　27
Origen　113, 158
orthodoxy. See theology, orthodox
Otto, Rudolf　23
pan(en)theism　24
paradoxical identity　28, 40, 50,
　　83, 98–99, 146, 148
parousia　7–8, 11
Paul (Pauline)　33–37, 39,
　　48, 56, 59, 62–65, 68–69,
　　72, 91–93, 122, 137
philosophy　10, 48–49,
　　122–23, 131
Pine, Lisa 130
plurality　11–12

presence-at-hand. *See* objective presence
preunderstanding   80–82
Quenstedt, Johannes Andreas   41
radical obedience   57
Rahner, Karl   83n51
reason   3, 32, 43–44, 49, 74
    See also science
Reformation   39, 113–14
ressourcement   142–43
revelation   17–18, 46, 49–50, 57–60, 63, 77, 81–82, 84, 95–99, 114
    and myth   103–5, 138
    and scripture 72, 74, 115, 126
righteousness
    alien   40–41
    imputed   39–40
    infused   39–41
Ritschl, Albrecht   4, 149
Roman Church (Roman Catholicism)   39, 113
Ross, Hugh   124
Rowe, C. Kavin   76
rule of faith (*regula fidei*)   77, 142–43
Sachkritik. See content criticism
salvation   33, 56, 65, 68, 78–79, 82, 84n54, 97, 103, 114, 122, 151–52
sanctification   39–40
Schleiermacher, Friedrich   4, 149
scholasticism. *See* theology, scholastic
Schweitzer, Albert   5, 6n10, 14, 92
science   43–44, 54–55, 60, 67–68, 86, 106, 113
    distinction from myth 102–4, 109–10
    and scripture   124–27

scripture
    cultural/historical context of 12, 107
    and historical consciousness 87–88
    and kerygma/revelation 17n9, 72–74, 77, 104, 115–16
    meaning of   112–13, 115, 117
    subject matter of   116–17
    otherness of   11–12, 14
    See also interpretation
security   11–12, 41–43, 47, 114, 136–40, 143–44
self-understanding   52–61, 67, 70, 72–75, 79–83, 120, 148
    as being outside ourselves   59
    as believing understanding 71
    natural   81
    as unconscious/unreflective 79–80, 82–83
secularization   90
sin   33, 35, 47–48, 58, 70, 81, 103, 121, 123, 135, 151
Soden, Hans von   129
Spirit   34–35, 37–39, 42, 47, 77, 122
Steinmetz, David   141
stoicism   135–36
subjectivism   131
subjectivity   114
subject matter (*Sache*)   116–20, 123
supernaturalism   4, 9, 104–5
theology
    apophatic   50
    dialectical   14–31, 48, 60, 108, 110

existential 21–23
hermeneutical 12, 109
historical nature of 22, 88–89
liberal 4, 8, 14–17, 20, 30–31,
48–50, 67–69, 92, 95,
108–10, 149, 151
natural 57, 81, 95
neoorthodox 14n1
New Testament 33, 71, 73,
75, 79
object of 23, 29
orthodox 49–50, 67,
69, 88, 113, 138–41
and philosophy 122–23
postliberal 141
as proclamation 21
of religions 78, 83–84
scholastic 20, 41, 113
systematic 75
theonomy 140
Thurneysen, Eduard 15
Tillich, Paul 15, 82, 89
tradition 74, 76–77, 88, 94, 113,
142–43
transcendence. *See* God, as
wholly other; immanence
and transcendence
translation 4, 71, 74,
107, 117, 121–28, 143
Troeltsch, Ernst 88
truth 9, 20–21, 33, 44, 74, 131,
134
and correspondence 126
general/timeless 54, 70, 74
of myth 103–5, 109,
118
universalism 84n54
verbal plenary inspiration 113
virtue 39–40
Vorhandenheit. See objective
presence

Walton, John 125–27
Watson, Francis 112
Weiss, Johannes 2, 4–6, 14
world-picture (*Weltbild*) 11, 58,
73, 104–11, 118–19, 121,
127
worldview (*Weltanschauung*) 28,
70
Wright, N. T. 10, 88

Printed in Great Britain
by Amazon